AGATA TOROMANOFF

NORDIC HOMES

SCANDINAVIAN ARCHITECTURE IMMERSED IN NATURE

Lannoo

TABLE OF CONTENTS

006
Introduction

008
Denmark

048
Sweden

148
Norway

202
Finland

244
Index

INTRODUCTION

In symbiosis with nature

Passion for nature and the importance of connecting with it are illustrated by the Nordic concept of spending time outdoors, called 'friluftsliv', which translates to 'open-air living'. In the 19th century it was widely popularised by the Norwegian playwright Henrik Ibsen as a special way to achieve both physical and mental well-being. The goal of getting outdoors and experiencing the beauty of an untouched natural environment, even quite remotely, is not difficult to achieve in the Nordic countries, as the populations are not large and the land is enormous. As part of everyone's life, spending time in nature is keenly practised as a daily routine, regardless of the time of year, even if the best season is the summer, when the sun never sets in certain regions. Seeing the lush plants, drawing from the power of the forests and enjoying views of water all inspire joy and help maintain balance and good health.

The role of suburban houses and summer retreats becomes important, and they are quite popular for the ultimate getaways into nature, thus they pose interesting design challenges for architects. Additionally, as the Nordic region leads the world among the most environmentally friendly countries, sustainability is another essential element of each architectural realisation. In this awe-inspiring journey across the Nordic countries in pursuit of the perfect Nordic home, we present the most inspiring realisations of the leading architectural studios, realised in the last couple of years. Houses growing from the striking landscapes initiate interesting dialogues with their natural surroundings, featuring skilfully blurred inside–outside boundaries. The architects enhance the celebration of nature by smoothly blending the architecture into the natural environment to maximise the reconnection of the inhabitants to Mother Earth.

Built in symbiosis with nature and following the rules of sustainability, these designs demonstrate exemplary uses of organic materials and natural light. These original volumes, integrated into the context, enclose spacious yet cosy interiors. Rich in textures and quiet in terms of colour palette, they offer aesthetic and comfortable living spaces. Thanks to generous openings they invite the landscape inside – some even create the feeling of being suspended in the middle of nature through glazed walls or cantilevered elements. The ingenious ideas of the architects both enhance the functionality of the spaces and allow residents to draw from the beauty and calmness of nature. Our selection of 30 stunning houses defines the contemporary Nordic home and demonstrates architecture that neither dominates nor competes with nature. What we can experience is the harmonious co-existence of both human-made and natural environments, in concert, improving the quality of life and transforming the everyday into a sensational experience.

Denmark

"Designing the house as being a part of nature"

Skagen Klitgård
PAX ARCHITECTS / 2021

While Skagen is known for being the furthest point in the north of Denmark, its traditional architecture, especially houses constructed in Skagen's Black Period with charred wood from shipwrecks, was a great inspiration for the PAX Architects studio. The most striking element is certainly the massive pitched roof covered in straw, which blends the volume into the grassy terrain. This summer house was built for a family of three generations, which required a programme combining the common spaces with separate areas under one continuous roof, so that each member of the family can freely enjoy time alone or moments together. The changing height of the ceiling, which also has an acoustic function, helps to define these zones and create their completely different atmospheres.

SKAGEN KLITGÅRD

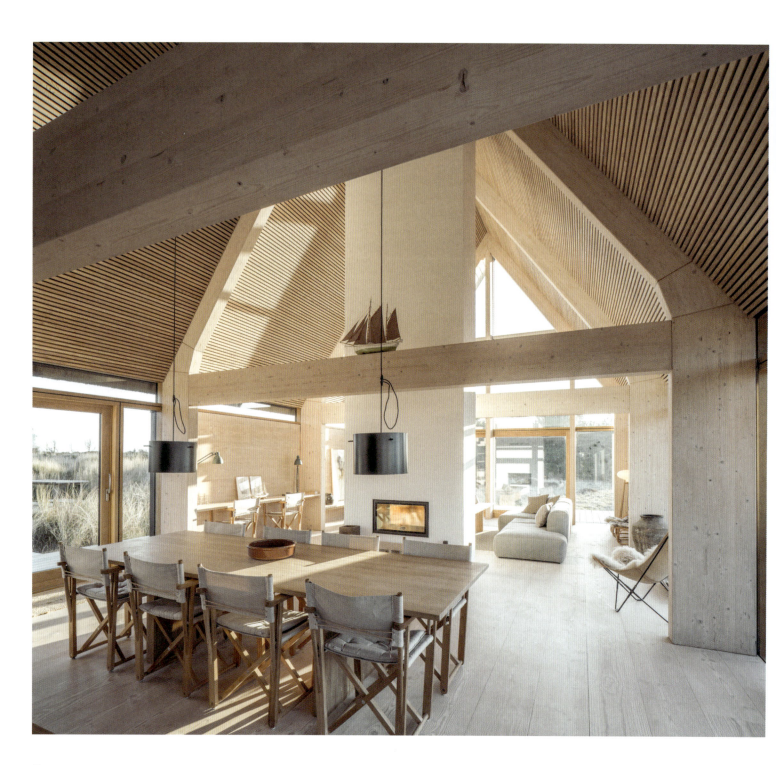

The architects' goal was to maintain a visual connection between various areas of the house, which are fluidly interconnected yet also subtly divided, like by a cupboard-filled wall or a fireplace. "The idea was to offer uninterrupted views along the long façades of the house, to bind the house together, but also to its surroundings," they explain. The natural colour palette in the warmly embracing interiors creates a visual continuum with the surroundings, enhanced by the generous windows set in thick oak frames. Built of sustainably sourced timber, the impressive structure of the house not only celebrates the beauty of wood but also plays with its textures. The straw-covered roof is equally tactile inside and distinctively accentuates the integrated quality of the interiors, filled with natural light.

SKAGEN KLITGÅRD

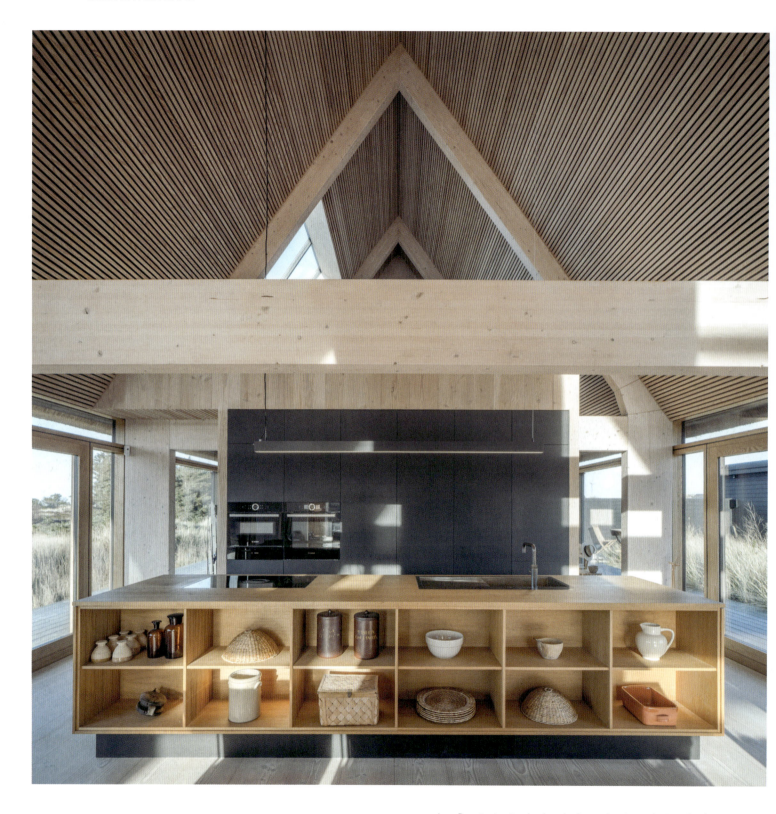

Despite its simple plan, the house has been designed with the perfect balance between open spaces and more intimate areas, with most of the interiors having access to natural light through the largely glazed walls. The centrally located kitchen is the heart of the house.

"Movement through the house as a spatially contrasting narrative"

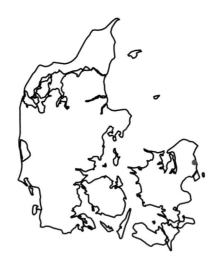

Kildeskovsvej
VALBÆK BRØRUP ARCHITECTS / 2023

Informed by the brick-made residential district from the beginning of the 20th century, the house employs the traditional material in a purely contemporary way. The originally shaped, geometric volume presents an eye-catching play between solid and transparent, with its terracotta-hued window frames matching the colour of the bricks and thus enhancing the monolithic nature of the volume. "We wanted to create a hyper-modern residence, but with clear references to the old villas and the context in which the project is situated," muse the architects, who turned the house into an inspiring dialogue between the inside and outside. The openings extend up to the ceiling on both levels, opening the interiors to the landscape as well as the sky. This direct connection with nature throughout the house provides a feeling of comfort and well-being.

KILDESKOVSVEJ

KILDESKOVSVEJ

> The well-lit kitchen as well as the dining area are located in the central part of the house, with views of both garden areas. The glazed wall can be entirely opened to erase the border between inside and outside.

DENMARK

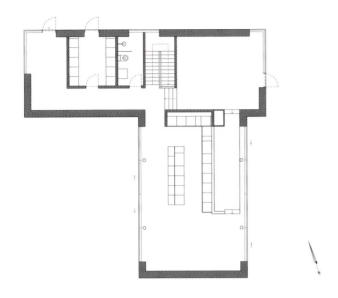

A very special area in the house is the so-called tea room located on the ground floor, in a corner of the house that is entirely glazed. The minimalist furnishings and full view of the garden make it a contemplative space. The intention of the architects when planning the spaces was to make the movement through various zones a spatially contrasting narrative. Each space of the ground level is strongly defined by its function and related to the sloping plot that the house centrally occupies. A smooth yet not always direct connection with the garden encircling the villa adds lightness to the brick volume. The top floor, dedicated to the private areas, continues the pared-down interior design and thus shifts the whole focus onto the sculptural brick shape.

The windows on the upper level offer a glimpse of the lush greenery of the garden as well as opening the private rooms to a view of the sky, significantly enhancing the sense of space.

"A commitment to genuine materiality that engages the senses"

Heatherhill Beach House
NORM ARCHITECTS / 2024

This holiday home, designed with great respect for the environment and in a symbiotic relationship with it, connects its inhabitants to the surrounding nature through its conscientiously designed spaces. The architects aimed to make the beauty of the surrounding landscapes a constant element of the various interiors, to enrich the interiors as much as the inhabitants' experience of the context. "From sunrise to sunset, the changing light and moods of nature become an integral part of everyday life," they emphasise. Each architectural and design decision is reflective and thoughtful, resulting in a timeless and calming effect, perfectly in line with the way the natural context of the plot affects the senses. The Heatherhill Beach House had been envisioned for an immersive experience and to become the ultimate retreat to ease the stress of everyday life.

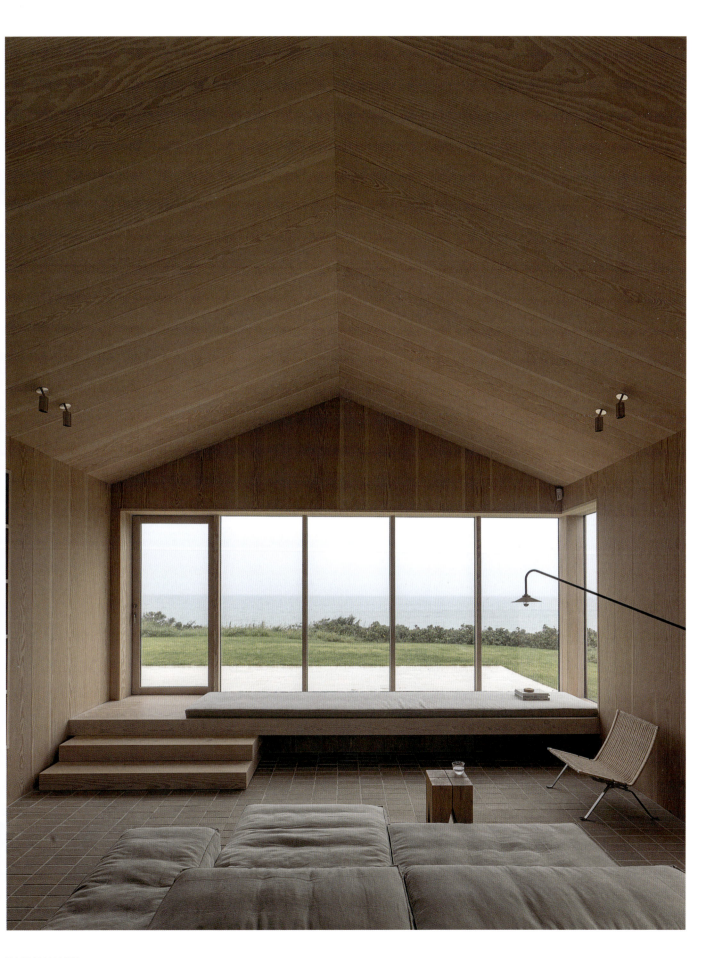

HEATHERHILL BEACH HOUSE

The colour of wood that will naturally weather with time and the fact that the roofs are covered with greenery ensure that the house perfectly harmonises with the context, even despite its distinctive barn-like shape.

HEATHERHILL BEACH HOUSE

The minimalist furnishing of the interiors puts the emphasis on the materiality of the structural elements and tactile impressions. There is nothing superfluous in the rooms – only essentials, highlighted by an honest attitude towards the materials and craftsmanship. Two axes connect the spaces for different functions in a continuous manner, with interesting interventions like the sunken living room with its stunning panorama. The views framed by each space offer unique experiences and a pleasant continuation between the inside and outside, while the timber-clad walls and ceilings create a cosy envelope for enjoyable family holidays. The architects' idea of long views throughout the interiors finds its continuation towards the exterior thanks to numerous openings with vistas in different directions, yet another element that binds the architecture and landscape together. While the material choice pays tribute to and reflects the natural world, the architects also celebrated Danish heritage by selecting a traditional brick floor for part of the interiors. Quintessentially sustainable, the structure sits on the previous house plot to reduce the impact on the land to a minimum.

HEATHERHILL BEACH HOUSE

The windows in various rooms take numerous shapes and are set deep in the walls – they are thus reminiscent of photo frames, perfectly capturing selected scenes, rather than simple openings.

"Allowing the surrounding natural landscape to take centre stage"

Vipp Cold Hawaii Guesthouse
HAHN LAVSEN / 2024

The sandy dunes of Cold Hawaii, in Thy National Park, Denmark (the country's largest national park), provide dramatic scenery for this simple yet striking guesthouse envisioned by the architects Caroline Hahn and Ebbe Lavsen. A transformation of an old fisherman's cottage facing the North Sea and dating back to the early 1900s gives this traditional architecture an interesting contemporary twist. The remote location in the magnificently raw coastal landscape inspired the architects to open the house entirely onto the hypnotising and relaxing surroundings. The local vernacular architecture, which in the past mainly protected the house's inhabitants from the strong western winds, has been reinvented through large openings that celebrate the views, with the grand glazed end gable facing the seafront in the main role. The architects decided to use a reduced palette of only five materials: aerated concrete, wood, stainless steel, glass and brick, to achieve, as they explain, honest expression and intentional rawness.

VIPP COLD HAWAII GUESTHOUSE

The sofa in the living room is perfectly harmonised with the windows, opening up the space to three different sides and creating the illusion of sitting in the middle of the dunes.

DENMARK

"Defined by three main sections divided by four open gables, the layout guides the eye to nature's panorama," muses Vipp, the Danish design brand who commissioned the conversion. The house has two floors and three double bedrooms, with some additional sleeping space possibilities. Other spaces include two bathrooms, a utility room, and interconnected living and kitchen areas. Julie Cloos Mølsgaard, the interior designer responsible for the project, selected furniture and objects with strong character and craftsmanship, in a limited material scheme for the finest effect. The tactile experience, intensified by the soft calming tones that are paired with the hues of the surrounding dunes, brings the context harmoniously together – the architecture as well as the interiors – and makes the best of the endless views of untamed nature and the secluded location in each part of the house.

VIPP COLD HAWAII GUESTHOUSE

The vivid kitchen area benefits from the generous traditional pitched roof to give the sense of an airy space filled with natural light. The aluminium kitchen as well as the furniture are from Vipp.

VIPP COLD HAWAII GUESTHOUSE

"In the midst of a clearing in the forest"

Lysal Pavilion
N+P ARKITEKTUR / 2023

"We strongly believe in the quality of solutions where form, function and construction go hand in hand," state the architects of N+P, who designed this villa in the middle of a forest in the scenic Lundby Krat area to the southeast of Aalborg, Denmark. The starting point of the vision was to create a transparency that would blend the residential area with its natural surroundings. This integration has been achieved through the largely glazed walls and adapting the shape to the sloping terrain. The pavilion rests on a concrete base with two wood-clad volumes atop it, tied together with a horizontal metal band. The elegant combination of materials gives the house a timeless look.

The profile of the house is perfectly in tune with the topography of the wooded plot.

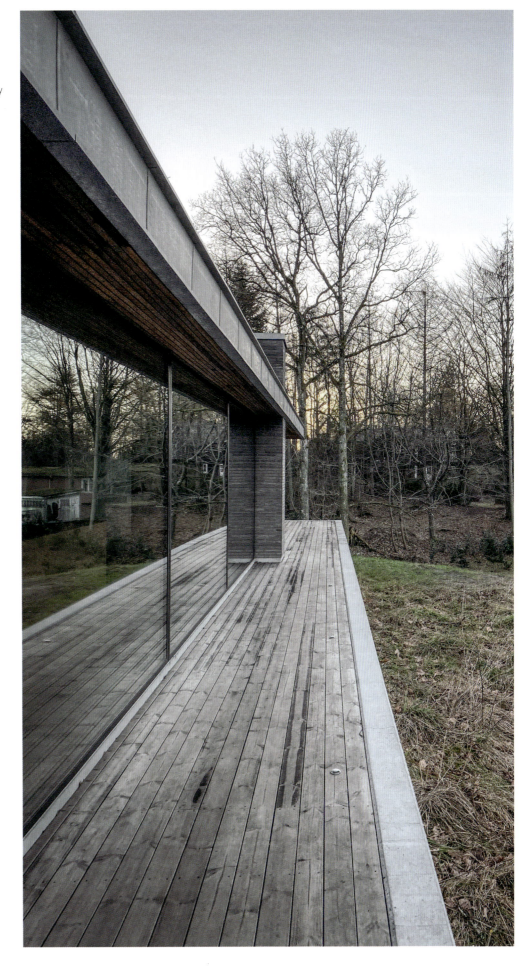

LYSAL PAVILION

LYSAL PAVILION

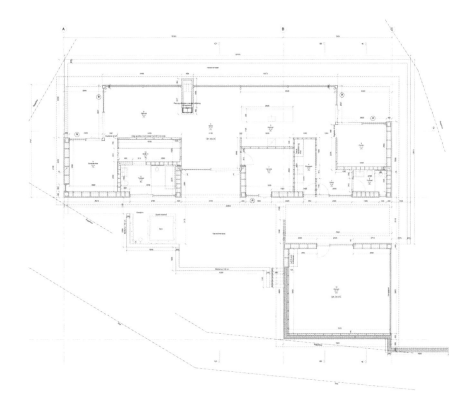

The nature enveloping the house, with its changing colours throughout the year and light throughout the day, becomes a vital part of the main living area, which is one open space, interrupted only by small elements like the kitchen island and the fireplace. The continuous space reflects the perspective from outside of the windows, while the transparent façade facing the landscape creates an illusion – as if the house were floating gently above the ground – which visually reduces the impact of the human-made structure on the natural site. The architects wanted to create a fusion of purely contemporary design with the beauty of the wooded landscape, an effect which is not only the result of their smart integration of the volume into the silhouette of the terrain but also of their ample use of wood on the outer shell.

Sweden

"Sheltered by the treetops"

Villa Strömma
ANDRÉNFOGELSTRÖM / 2022

The villa sits amid the dream-like scenery of a cliff with views overlooking the canal of Strömma in the Stockholm archipelago. Additionally, the plot is filled with lush vegetation that creates a pleasantly calming envelope. Preserving the old oaks and pines on the site was the main objective for the architects. Their green foliage contrasts nicely with the black-wood volumes of the house. Each of the five volumes is dedicated to a different function. While the generously spaced middle one houses the kitchen and living space, and opens to the garden to benefit from views of the water, the private rooms are located in the eastern volume. Interestingly, the arrangement of the parts is adjusted to the topography of the terrain in a highly original way, so that the spatial experience is highlighted, even upon entering.

VILLA STRÖMMA

The living area is literally bathed in natural light, with transparent walls that additionally enhance the feeling of space.

VILLA STRÖMMA

"The house is accessed from the upper level, a dramatic entrance via a footbridge that spans a crevice," note the architects from AndrénFogelström studio. They have envisioned the villa as a composition of three parts arranged around a Japanese-style garden, in harmony with the exposed stones of the cliff. An interesting mix of contrasting materials are positioned next to each other: the black wood panelling of the exterior shell of the volumes, the solid wooden window frames in a lighter colour, the main entrance clad in copper, and the roof made of black metal. Another striking element is the slender steel construction of the cantilevered parts of the house, including the spacious terrace with waterside vistas. The landscape itself becomes part of the house's comfortable and cosy spaces.

Framed views of the vegetation embracing the house enrich the interiors by creating an atmosphere of calm, particularly cherished in private rooms.

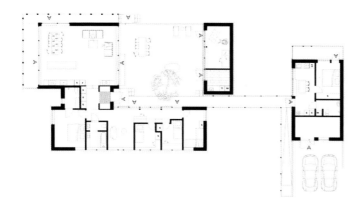

"The two houses can be experienced as independent parts"

Villa Timmerman
ANDREAS LYCKEFORS + JOSEFINE WIKHOLM / 2020

This sculptural, semi-detached house in a suburban residential area in the southwest of Gothenburg has been designed as the private home of the married architect couple Andreas Lyckefors and Josefine Wikholm. "It was a challenge to create a semi-detached house with equal qualities on both ends as they naturally face different directions," remarks Andreas. Their main objective was to envision it so that both parts of the house got sunlight at all times of the day. Based on careful study of the local weather conditions as well as the trajectory of the sun, the architects programmed the volume in the most optimal way. The flow of light also influenced the floor plan, a challenging task due to the fact that the house sits on a slope.

VILLA TIMMERMAN

The openings in the living area ensure that there is ample natural light to animate the space for family get-togethers.

VILLA TIMMERMAN

The large staircase connecting all levels is built of ash wood with some deeper stair levels that form small sitting spaces.

VILLA TIMMERMAN

Their ambitious goal was to make the house grow with the family during all stages of life, which is why the architects decided to break up the typical function-separated room plan. Bedrooms and toilets are located on all floors, and the social room runs throughout the house. Small children can sleep close to their parents, while teenagers or guests can occupy their own floor. Villa Timmerman is made of semi-prefabricated wood with a pre-cut frame that was later mounted on site. The volume's outer cladding is striking, made of three grids of diagonal and vertical ribs that give the house a tactile quality. What intensifies the visual effect is the wood tar, a combination of black and brown pigment, which makes the façade appear different depending on the light.

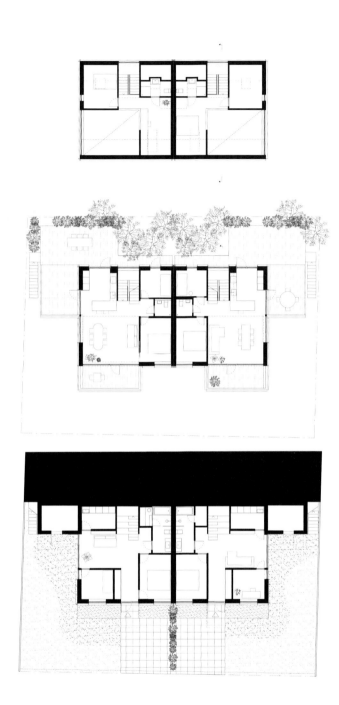

While the wooden roof that gives the volume a monolithic look has seamlessly integrated solar panels, the three-dimensional grid on the outer shell of the building acts as protection against the solar radiation as well as drifting rain.

"Far out in the archipelago of Stockholm"

Holiday Home
MARGEN WIGOW ARKITEKTKONTOR / 2019

This holiday home on an island in the archipelago of Stockholm, designed by Cecilia Margen Wigow and Per Wigow, is a complex of five buildings: the main house, guest house, a sauna, a boathouse with storage, and a garden shed. Integrated into the rocky plot in the midst of nature, they overlook a picturesque bay. "The roofs' slope has the same direction as the mountain shape and is covered with grass," explain the architects. The green roofs in combination with the low height smooth the fusion of the volumes into the natural environment.

HOLIDAY HOME

The façades are largely glazed to showcase views in numerous directions, while the solid parts that offer protection from weather conditions as well as privacy for holidaymakers are all clad in wooden panels painted black, which in a way makes all five buildings seem smaller in the island's panorama. In a stark contrast, the interiors are defined by pine plywood in a natural colour, which visually enlarges the spaces. This warm wooden wrap, complemented by elements in the neutral colour palette, results in nest-like indoor spaces. The remote location of the complex and semi-transparent structures inspire a reconnection with nature. As there is no electricity on the island, the buildings are heated by fireplaces, which adds yet another layer of charm when spending one's holidays there not only during the warm summertime.

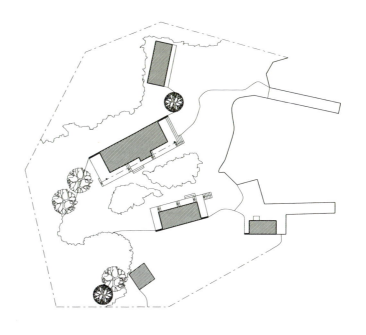

HOLIDAY HOME

> Adjusted to the rocky terrain, the interiors of the house are located on two levels, which also defines their functions.

The sitting area has a chimney to create a cosy atmosphere on colder days, as well as a panoramic window for enjoying views of the water while relaxing.

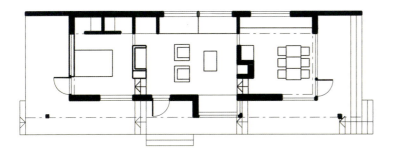

"A graceful pavilion half-hidden by deciduous trees"

Summerhouse Solviken
JOHAN SUNDBERG ARKITEKTUR / 2018

"Summerhouse Solviken is a treehouse, sheltered from the weather and wind with a generous view to the south," remarks Johan Sundberg. The architect's villa in the summer coastal retreat of Mölle, Sweden, is placed with a striking virtuosity. Protruding from a steep hill and hidden in the dense woodland overgrowing it, the geometric volume sits delicately on 12 steel pillars. Barely visible, they create a captivating optical illusion, especially intriguing given the volume's scale. Elevated to the level of the treetops, this ultramodern summer house enjoys exceptional views and offers an interesting spatial experience. In the first place, to enter it, one has to climb a steep set of stairs from the street level. From the balcony arranged along two of the façades, the inhabitants can enjoy the vistas and spend time outdoors surrounded by greenery, as if they were in a treehouse.

SUMMERHOUSE SOLVIKEN

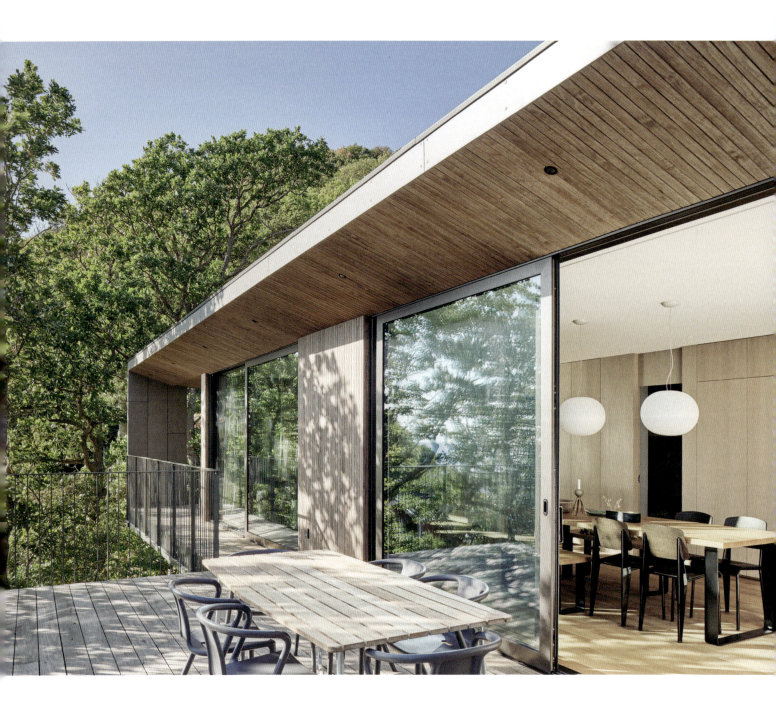

In addition to the balcony programmed along two façades, the dining area opens onto a spacious terrace – a scene for the play of shadows created by the foliage of tall trees.

The architect planned three bedrooms towards the north, and the common areas of the open-space kitchen, dining and living room to face the view in the front. As there are no corridors in the house, all zones are fluidly interconnected with several more intimate corners dedicated to relaxation. Oak wood is the material dominating the interiors – together with the sunlight coming in through the floor-to-ceiling windows, this creates a spacious and bright effect. The house is a simple yet pleasant area to enjoy holidays. The palette of colours both inside and outside is meant to place the architecture harmoniously into the context, like the idea of using green hues for elements like the façade boards, balcony railings and load-bearing parts. This intervention softens the distinctive geometry and makes the house visually vanish into the slope. The project was designed together with associate architect Itziar del Río Gómiz.

SUMMERHOUSE SOLVIKEN

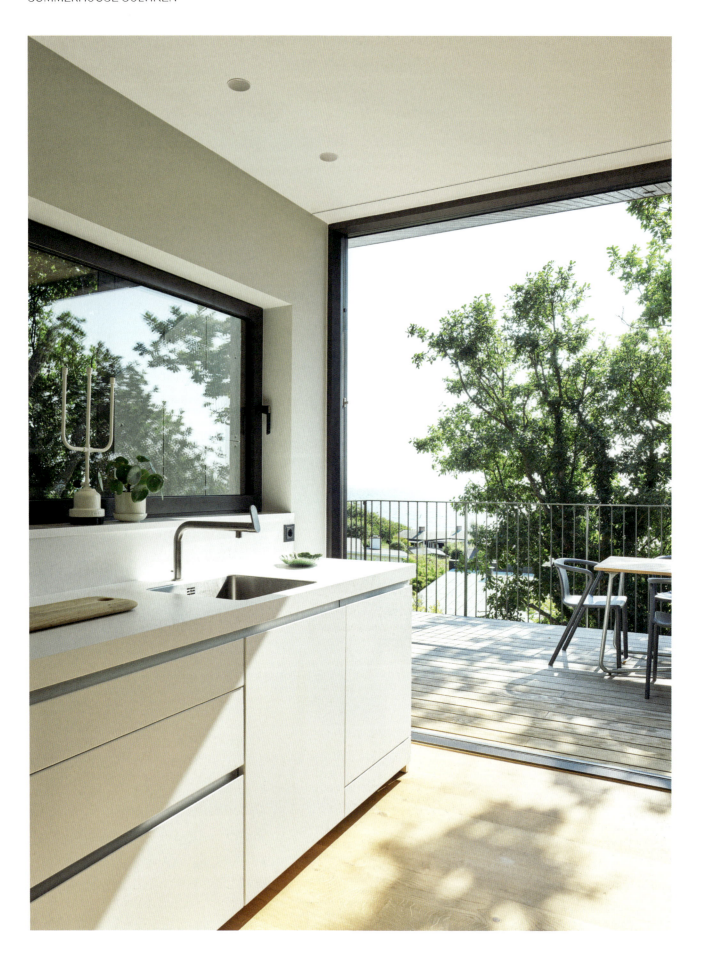

SUMMERHOUSE SOLVIKEN

The way this cubic volume is perched dramatically on a steep slope reduces the impact of the architecture on the land and places it in quite an unusual location, among the treetops.

"Small-scale structures blend seamlessly amidst the trees"

Yngsjö
JOHAN SUNDBERG ARKITEKTUR / 2023

Yngsjö, located on the shore of the Baltic Sea, offers a typically Nordic atmosphere for a summer retreat. Johan Sundberg designed this pavilion-style house on a hilly plot covered with pines. "The landscape here embraces a lack of meticulously landscaped gardens, opting instead for the dominance of the natural forest setting," emphasises the architect. The house clad in larch fits perfectly in this untamed environment. The compact and low volume is adjusted to the natural topography – the southern part with the entrance, kitchen and communal areas has direct contact with the ground, which enables smooth communication between the inside and outside. The private spaces are located in the northern part of the house, which sits on pillars and also initiates a dialogue with the surroundings, only in a different way.

YNGSJÖ

Each space, even the corridor, offers a glimpse of the surrounding natural context which also brings more natural light inside.

This relationship between all the interiors and the scenically wooded plot is amplified on all sides of the house by large openings. They seem to invite inhabitants to take a step outside to enjoy the natural beauty of the site with a culmination in the sheltered terrace connected with the living area that offers a nice, relaxing space, and is oriented in such a way that the inhabitants can enjoy the evening sun. Regardless of the weather, this lovely summer house offers a calming space where larch ceilings, floors and furniture create a harmonious family nest amid Nordic nature. The subdued palette of hues in the interior design and lack of superfluous furnishings as well as the numerous openings all form the perfect combination for well-being. This project was envisioned in collaboration with Staffan Rosvall.

YNGSJÖ

Thanks to the lightweight structure and flat, large base on which the house is posed on one side, there is a small terrace encircling the volume and the structure seems to be floating just above the level of the plot.

"The overall sense of a gradual transition between house and landscape"

Field House
LOOKOFSKY ARCHITECTURE / 2020

This composition of originally arranged wooden volumes with individual A-line roofs is surprising at first glance, with its geometric presence in the middle of a grassy plot. The way it has been realised, however, binds it to the landscape. The architect, David Lookofsky, drew from the local typology of fishing villages and small farmhouses on the Swedish island of Fårö. He also took inspiration from the area's traditional method of roof cladding with wood boards, using denser larch boards instead of the traditional pine wood cladding. The idea was to create a natural external skin that would change over time from the effects of the atmospheric conditions and eventually evolve into a shimmering, silver grey tone. The house can also evolve structurally, as new volumes can be freely added to accommodate the changing needs of the inhabitants and enhance the shifted scheme, still without dominating the natural environment.

FIELD HOUSE

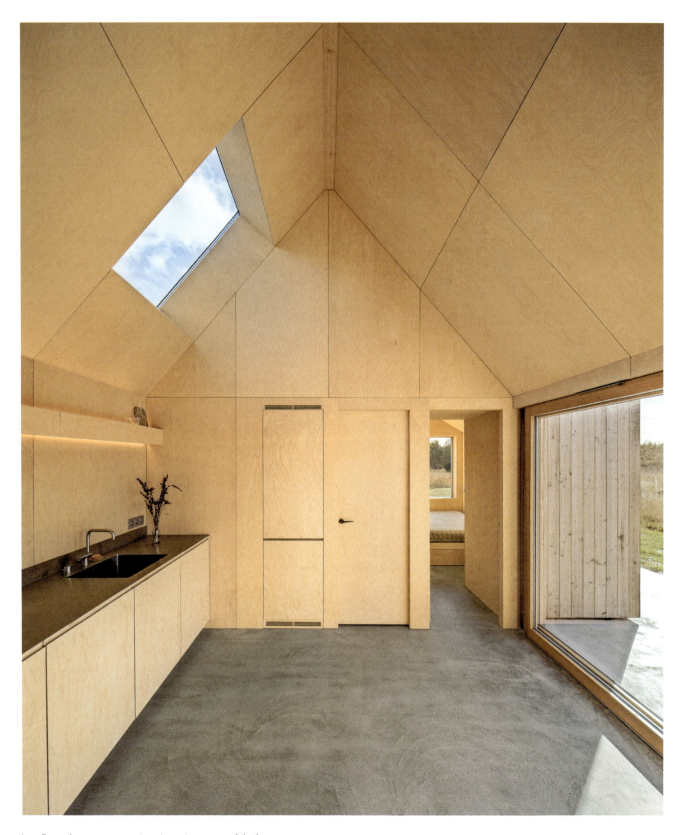

Several generous openings in various parts of the house are perfect sources of natural light and break up the solidity of the interior walls.

FIELD HOUSE

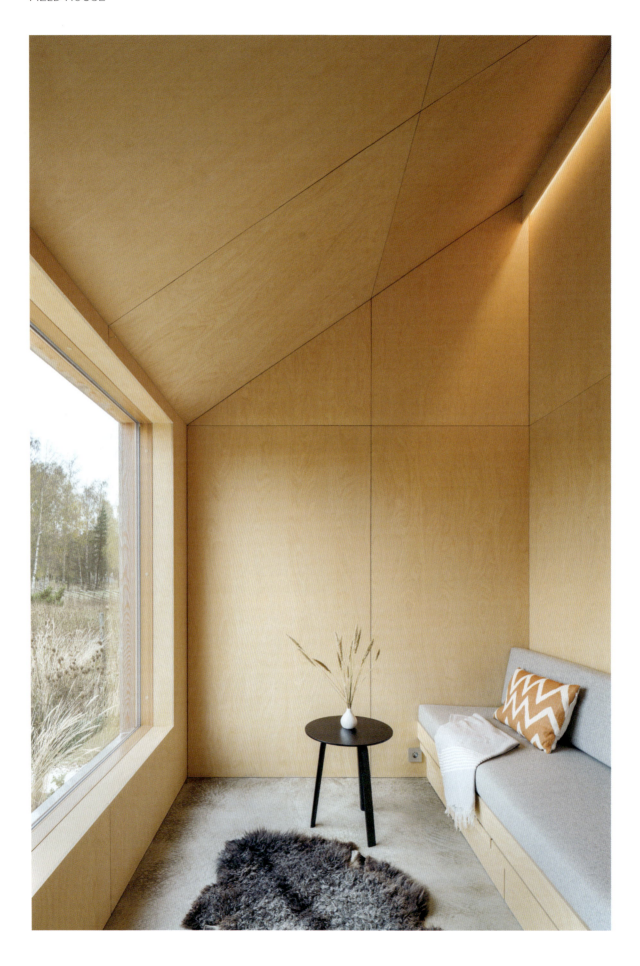

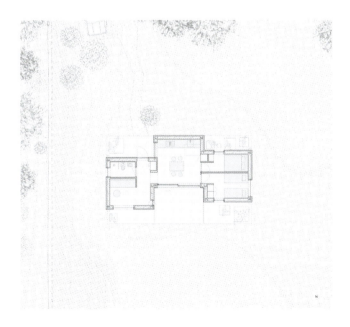

The interiors are modestly sized yet organised comfortably. A warm atmosphere is achieved with birch plywood cladding that envelops all the walls as well as the tall ceiling, with both storage and some of the furniture seamlessly integrated into the walls to save space. Each of the volumes has a different function – one houses a bedroom, the middle one is the common space, and the third a contemplative reading room. "Frameless windows and a large sliding door create focused views towards the field and bring selected parts of the landscape and the sky inside each room of the house," the architect explains. The volumes are identical in their footprint but not in placement nor in height, which allowed the architect to establish different relationships between the house, its inhabitants and the surroundings. This playful arrangement and lack of symmetry resonates with the character of this summer house – traditional with a modern twist.

FIELD HOUSE

"A home that is quiet and deferential to the context"

Dalarö House
OLSON KUNDIG / 2019

The Swedish house designed by the American architect Tom Kundig has an interesting combination of influences. The project not only celebrates the beautiful landscapes of the island of Dalarö in the Stockholm archipelago but also pays tribute to the local historical architecture. In particular, the new summer house is located just next to the historic Strindberg Cottage, which has been restored by its current owners as a guest house. This proximity inspired certain elements in the ultracontemporary villa, like the characteristic windows that create an interesting dialogue between old and new. The living area with comfortable lounge, kitchen and dining space take up the central part of the volume, which is accompanied by two smaller wings with bedrooms and bathrooms. All spaces have been envisioned with large windows, providing views and a direct connection with natural surroundings inspiring the interaction.

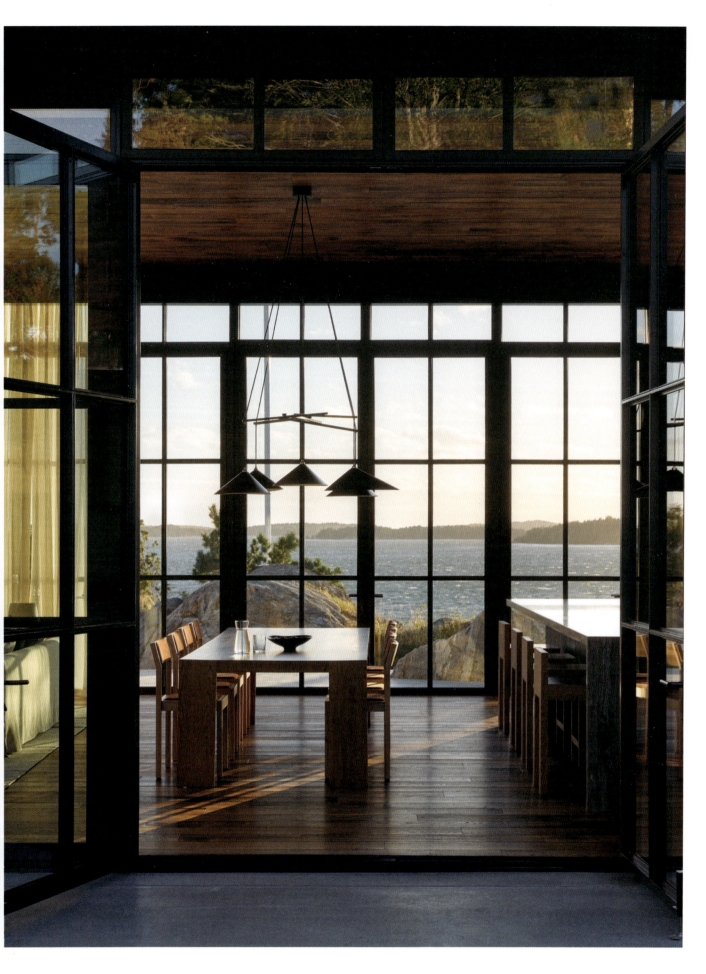

DALARÖ HOUSE

Most striking is that this holiday home has been incorporated into the massive granite rocks on the plot, making them part of the structure, while the large windows connect the interiors with stunning views of the coast.

The private and social spaces are divided by a massive yet highly aesthetic wall of exposed concrete, which demonstrates an original approach to the selection and juxtaposition of materials. The architects' way of combining wood, metal and concrete is quite intriguing. This emphasis on materiality, straight lines and some smoothness creates a stark contrast to the topography of the site, in particular the rugged rocks. In the pursuit of creating a quiet retreat for warm and bright summer days, the architects used a dark colour palette, unusual for Scandinavian traditions, with a rather elegant result. Interestingly, a local pigment of red hue called falun red, typical for the region's villages and homes, has been used to amplify the entrance and harmonise the new architecture with the neighbouring guest house.

DALARÖ HOUSE

"Immersive connection with its natural surroundings"

Sjöparken
NORM ARCHITECTS / 2024

The unique floating village of seven villas that make up the Sjöparken retreat has been designed with a harmonious coexistence between luxurious living and the Swedish landscape. When speaking about this project, the architects do not refer to it as constructing a building but rather as crafting an experience, which essentially resonates with the spirit of the place. The wooden cladding of the traditionally shaped volumes, topped with green roofs, truly exemplifies this approach. "We wanted to create something that could stand out and be spectacular in the most understated and natural way possible," comment the architects, who drew inspiration from various notions, ranging from Nordic simplicity and the timeless traditions of Japanese design to the tropical allure of resort living.

SJÖPARKEN

SJÖPARKEN

Surrounded by the beech forests of Halland, the lake with sunken swimming pools beneath its surface is an expansive jetty for seven houses with four rooms each, with interconnecting transparent corridors. Their interiors, bathed in natural colours and tactile materials mirroring the natural elements, offer comfort and well-being. All spaces have been envisioned in a perfect balance between intimate, cosy areas and blurring the inside–outside boundaries. While wooden elements, particularly the oak cladding, and soft textiles create relaxation zones, sizeable openings highlight areas that initiate dialogue with the site. The light filtered through the spaces has an essential role in animating the interiors. The pared-down aesthetic of the rooms offers calm and peace, as does the interaction with the surrounding nature.

SJÖPARKEN

The houses blend seamlessly into the site, including through their direct connection with water, the surface of which becomes a continuation of the terrace and continues on to the tranquil view of the lake.

"An origami-like pleated and rotated volume"

House on a Hill
THAM & VIDEGÅRD ARKITEKTER / 2022

"We envisioned the house as reduced to pure structure where indoor and outdoor spaces mix and let the emphasis remain on the scenery outside," state the architects. Although a concrete volume is quite uncommon for a typical Nordic house, set in this specific landscape, it looks particularly striking. It occupies a dream plot on a wooded slope on the water, with fantastic vistas of the archipelago, and is located just a 20-minute drive from the centre of Stockholm. Interestingly, the architects compare the house to a lighthouse on exposed bedrock, and that is certainly accurate, especially from the perspective of the steep driveway. Entirely cast in concrete, the villa looks firm but not heavy, mainly thanks to its multifaceted shape, playing with a solid–transparent opposition, and it remains in a direct relationship with its environment.

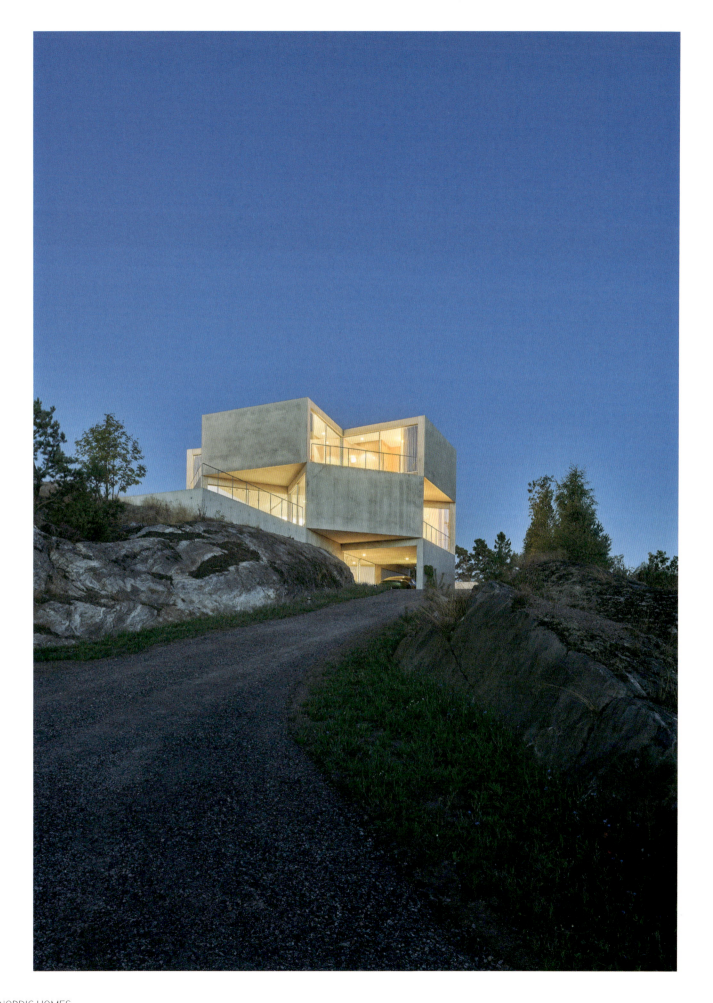

HOUSE ON A HILL

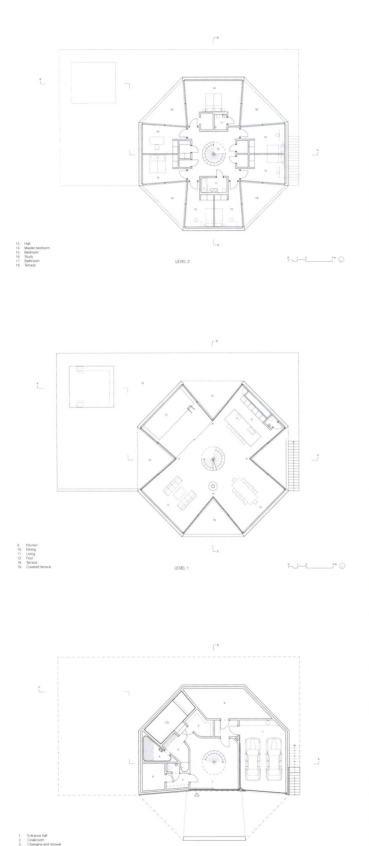

13. Hall
14. Master bedroom
15. Bedroom
16. Study
17. Bathroom
18. Terrace

LEVEL 2

9. Kitchen
10. Dining
11. Living
12. Pool
18. Terrace
19. Covered terrace

LEVEL 1

1. Entrance hall
2. Cloakroom
3. Changing and shower
4. Sauna
5. Wine cellar
6. Technical
7. Garage
8. Storage
(12. Pool)

ENTRANCE LEVEL

HOUSE ON A HILL

The centrally located spiral staircase is light and does not take up much space while smoothly interconnecting all levels.

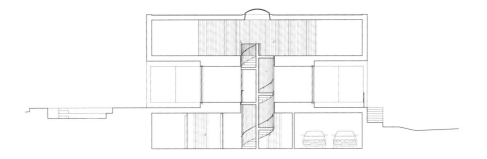

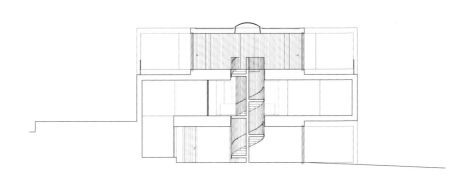

Because the volume is so inventively twisted, with a 45-degree rotation between each of the three levels, the architect made the landscape outside a point of reference for the interiors. The entrance and services are located on the souterrain level, the mid and main floors are dedicated to open-space common areas, and the bedrooms are planned at the top of the structure. While the solid walls provide privacy, panoramic windows in all rooms frame views facing different directions. Another element allowing the residents to fully enjoy the landscape is the inclusion of outdoor spaces on various levels – the terraces between the shifted volumes are well protected from the wind and also planned according to the trajectory of the sun. Dynamic on the outside, and well interconnected inside, the House on a Hill creates an ultramodern yet successful dialogue with nature.

HOUSE ON A HILL

A side effect of the playfully shaped volume are some of its unusually sized spaces, like this bedroom with a stunning vista through the entirely glazed wall.

"A house organised around a library in the shape of a book"

Library House
FRIA FOLKET, HANNA MICHELSON / 2022

This lightweight structure combining wood and glass wraps around a central patio in a series of four gable-roofed volumes. The choice of materials ensures that the house sits naturally on the plot at the edge of a sparse pine forest with a view of a lake. It has been constructed sustainably with plastic-free walls and roofs, insulated with flax fibres drawing on the local traditions, while the concrete-free foundation is made from recycled glass. The Library House is a tailor-made residence for a couple of entirely different professions, a ceramicist and a lawyer. As the name suggests, first and foremost was the need for a well-planned, and sufficiently large, library for the substantial book collection of the owners. The brief was more nuanced, however, and also required a house where both could work individually according to their different rhythms.

LIBRARY HOUSE

The interiors are furnished with pieces from the owners' previous house to reduce the environmental footprint, with Ikea's iconic 'Billy' bookshelf playing a vital role in the library.

LIBRARY HOUSE

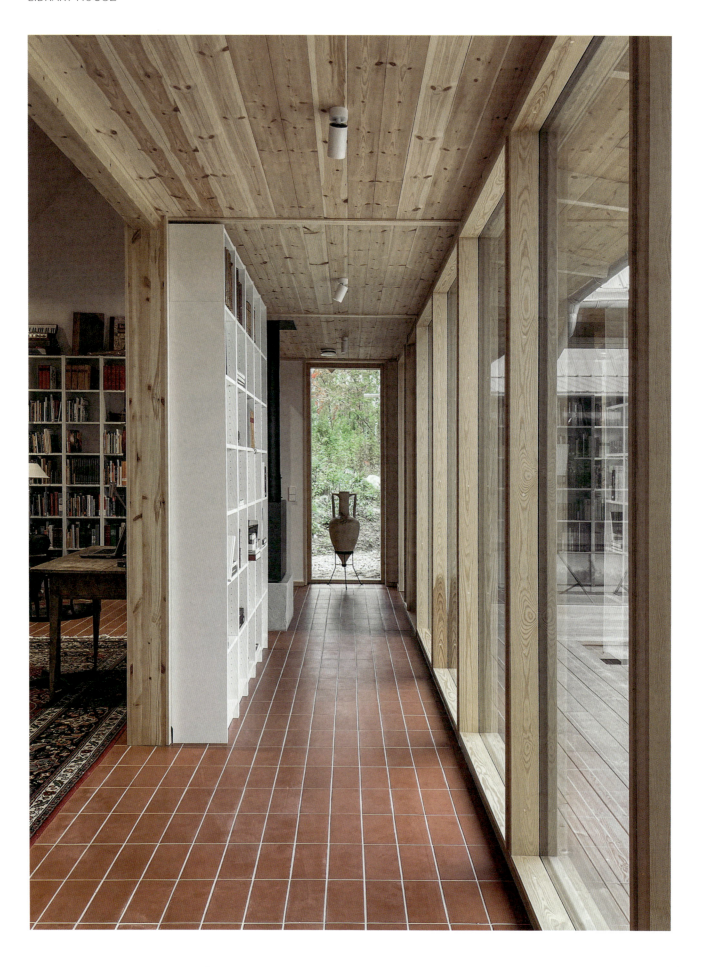

120

The owners' extensive book collection found a perfect home and has become the heart of the house, linking all sections of this multifunctional residence.

LIBRARY HOUSE

Only the south side facing the lake is transparent to communicate with the surroundings, while the other façades are solid with only selected views framed by openings.

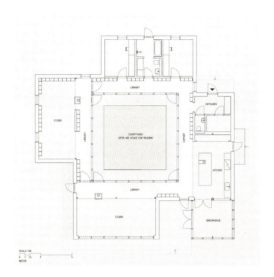

The architect Fria Folket's concept was to place the library at the heart of the house and transform it into the element linking all the buildings. The east volume, with a spacious greenhouse, has a cooking and gardening theme, the south volume is dedicated to arts and crafts, and the west one to law, science and music, while the north building features areas for relaxation. This diverse and ambitious programme is successful thanks to the fact that each section is coherent with the whole, yet separate – all subtly interconnected by the library framing the small courtyard. The courtyard also enhances communication throughout the home as it is accessible from all parts of the house. "The four houses are organised in the order of the sun's movement with the starting point of the house, i.e., the entrance, in line with the starting point of the day, in the east," explains the architect.

"To emphasise the building's sculptural qualities"

Simonsson House
CLAESSON KOIVISTO RUNE ARCHITECTS / 2021

As in other disciplines, in architecture, too, restrictions can often be the best driver of ingenious concepts. When designing this house just south of the Arctic Circle, Claesson Koivisto Rune Architects faced unusually strict regulations. The main challenge was posed by the height limit with a maximum of only 4.2 metres, which made the creation of the second floor problematic. The architects solved this by using a single pitched roof construction. "Since the building height for a single pitched roof is a calculated mean value around the house, the resulting building height could be kept within the regulations," they explain. The result functions within the restrictions and offers a comfortable living space but is also visually quite original. The main volume is juxtaposed with a smaller trapezoidal one housing a garage and a sauna. Facing opposite directions, they dynamise the overall shape.

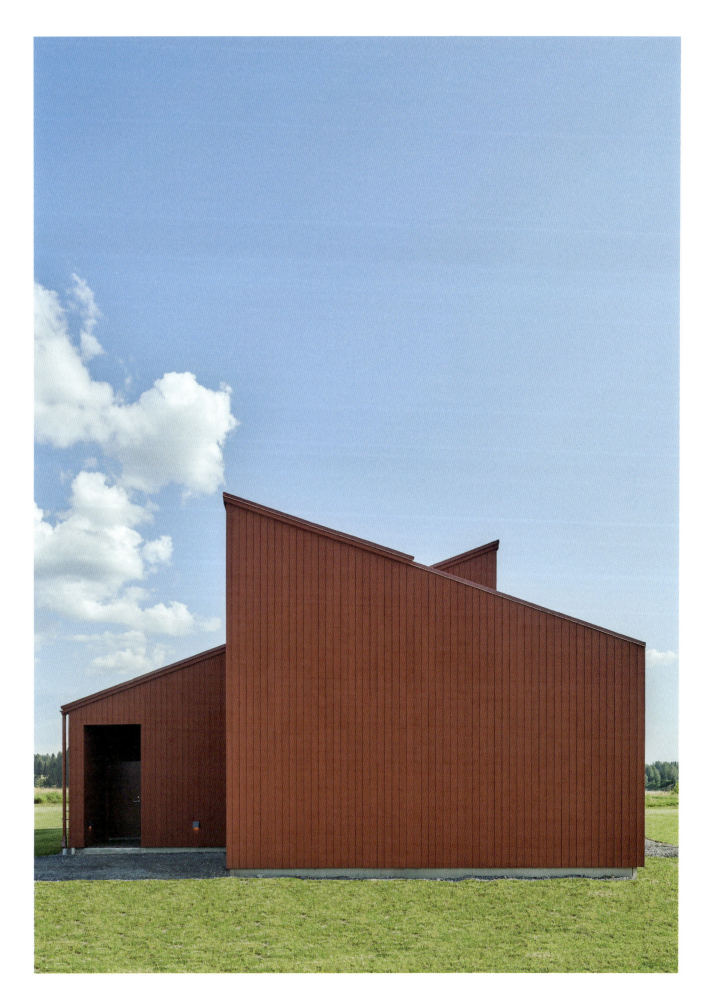

SIMONSSON HOUSE

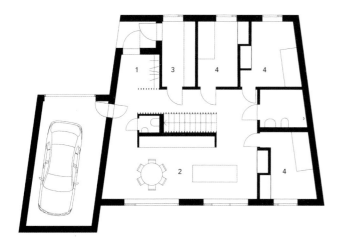
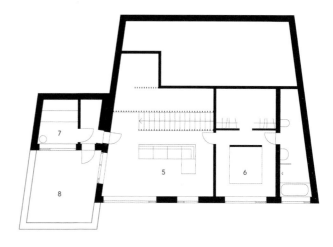

1. ENTRANCE
2. KITCHEN
3. LAUNDRY
4. BEDROOM

5. LIVING ROOM
6. MASTER BEDROOM
7. SAUNA
8. ROOF TERRACE

The site is bordered by trees along the Lule River, a major river in Sweden. The architects decided to pierce the side facing the river with numerous openings, as well as create a terrace on the roof of the garage to make the most of the striking views. Due to the slope, the ground floor accommodates the kitchen with a dining area and all the bedrooms, while the top floor, in the style of a mezzanine, creates a sitting area, visually enlarged by its massive windows and connection with the outdoor terrace. The interiors are designed in neutral colours, complementing the wooden elements like the ceiling, which contrasts with the distinctive outer shell. Here, the monolithic character is amplified by the red colour applied to all exterior surfaces, and not only to the roof as was stipulated by the local regulations.

SIMONSSON HOUSE

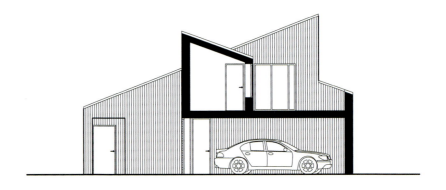

The sculptural form of the house allowed for the playful arrangement of openings, which break up the otherwise monolithic façade, oriented towards the river.

SIMONSSON HOUSE

"The little 'hamlet' of four scattered cubical buildings"

Johäll Getaway House
CLAESSON KOIVISTO RUNE ARCHITECTS / 2024

The secluded, wooded sloping shore of a lake is a plot as unusual as it is challenging for constructing a house. Yet, Claesson Koivisto Rune Architects have created a most ingenious 'getaway', and a perfectly functional holiday house, for a family of four. It consists of four parts – the main house, an annex, the sauna building and a garage – each located in a cube-like volume made of easily maintained galvanised steel and glass that elegantly balances on the steep bedrock. Surrounded by trees, the house disappears into the landscape, while its transparent structures invite the forest into the living spaces. The main design issue was not so much the nearly inaccessible site or its topography but the fact that the allowance mentioned a limit of 65 square metres, although with the possibility of some additional, smaller structures. "It was established from the outset to leave this enchanted nature as intact as possible, with a small visual imprint of the new," emphasises the studio.

JOHÄLL GETAWAY HOUSE

When spending time in the living room, inhabitants can have the impression of sitting outside in nature.

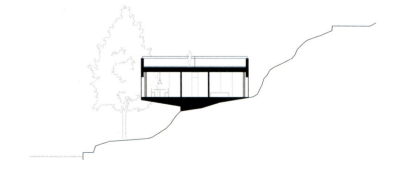

The architects came up with the surprising idea of breaking up the space into four constructions. The largest cube, the main house, has four interconnected yet somehow separated rooms, thanks to its rotated plan: the kitchen with the entrance, dining room, living room and one bedroom are all arranged around the central wooden cube containing a bathroom and storage area. This volume also offers a striking outdoor space on the extensive roof terrace, reachable through an outdoor spiral staircase. Additionally the twin-bedroom annex, sauna and carport, all cubic volumes, are strategically arranged on the slope – in parallel to each other as well as at a 45-degree angle in relation to the lake. As a result, the view can be admired from the perspectives of two different façades, dynamically facing the water.

JOHÄLL GETAWAY HOUSE

All glazed façades open onto the dreamy scenery with the effect that the house floats softly above the slope, providing an immersive experience.

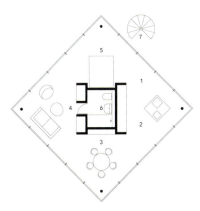

JOHÄLL GETAWAY HOUSE

"The materials of the house reflect the palette of the landscape"

South Loft
FRIA FOLKET, HANNA MICHELSON / 2021

South Loft is the second of four planned cabins envisioned by Hanna Michelson of Fria Folket studio, commissioned by Bergaliv Landscape Hotel, on the hillside of Åsberget Mountain in northern Sweden. The cabin features several substantial openings, mostly frameless for a stronger visual effect, as well as outdoor space in the form of a covered terrace facing a panorama of the Ljusnan river valley. "The wooden house is placed on a rock ledge balancing between the grandeur of the far landscape and the fine-tuned connection to the surrounding forest," explains the architect. All materials used in this project were chosen in harmony with the colours of the surrounding environment. The plastic-free construction draws from traditional Nordic building techniques, as the walls and roof are insulated with flax fibres.

SOUTH LOFT

In various parts of the house, the views are perfectly framed, with some sitting or lying areas positioned next to the openings for enjoying the landscape in tranquillity.

The interior is a multifunctional open space under a very tall half-pitched roof, allowing for a cosy sleeping loft in the mezzanine-like space. In the heart of the house, the main room with two large windows has been equipped with a bench and elevated floor which can be used for eating, sleeping, practising yoga or simply contemplating the vistas. The architect, inspired by the quiet natural surroundings, designed a minimalist space that is easy to rearrange throughout the day and can thus be used in many different ways. The lack of superfluous furnishings enhances the meditative quality of the space and evokes the stillness of the landscape outside of the windows. Wood in various textures and natural hues warmly embraces the guests of the South Loft.

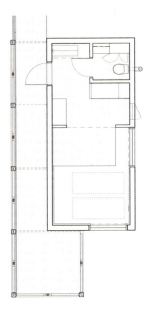

The living space in the South Loft has been designed in a very functional way to make the best of the compact interiors, embraced by the warm wood in natural colours.

SOUTH LOFT

The structure of the house has been elevated above the rocky slope to reduce the impact on the land to a minimum, but this has also enhanced the views.

"Besides being beautiful, the off-cuts are low in embodied carbon"

Saltviga House
KOLMAN BOYE ARCHITECTS / 2022

This charming holiday home enveloped by forest on the Norwegian southeastern coastline has been constructed from oak and Douglas off-cuts from Dinesen's floor production. Elements that would normally be used as firewood create a multilayer cladding pattern, accentuated – and fastened – with more than 20,000 stainless steel screws. What is essential in this inventive concept is that the production leftovers are naturally low in embodied carbon, and thus offer a good alternative to many other building materials. "By combining ennobled timber scraps with a reassessment of historical building vocabularies, the Saltviga House employs an updated architectural language of resource efficiency," remark the architects. This meticulously applied external shell will weather with time and blend in even more with the surrounding trees.

SALTVIGA HOUSE

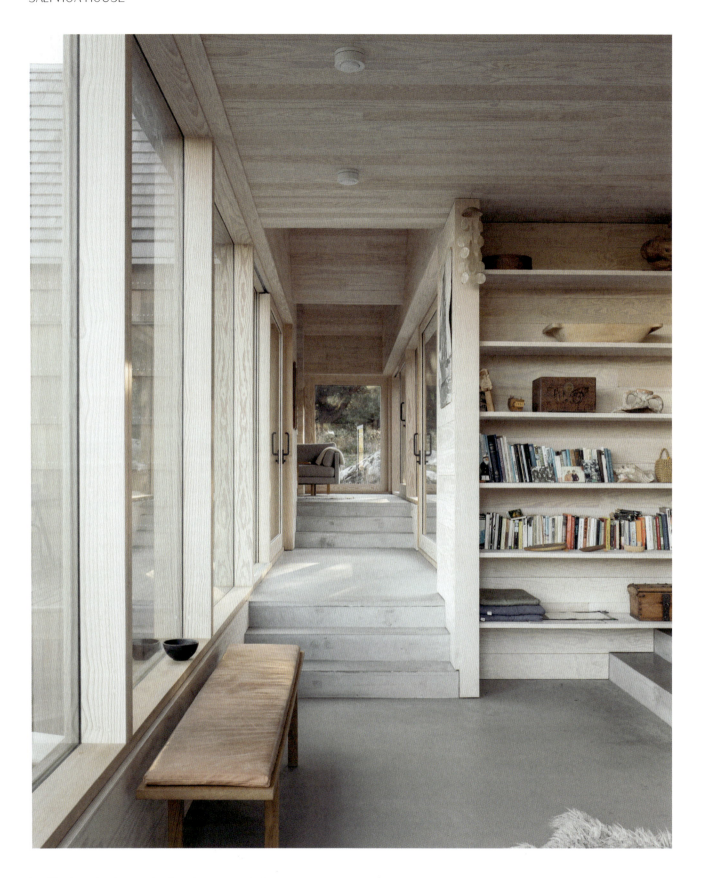

Thanks to the changing levels and numerous windows in various directions, moving through the house can be a way of experiencing the surrounding landscape.

SALTVIGA HOUSE

The perfect fusion of the house with the context is not merely visual but is also the result of the way the structure has been adjusted to the rocky foundation. As a principle, the architects insisted on perfect adaptation to rather than intervention into the terrain. As a result, the three volumes are located on five different levels, with the central hallway offering views throughout the entire house. This arrangement, together with numerous and generous openings, enhances one's experience of the surroundings while moving between spaces. The interiors are semi-transparent to breathe in the landscape, but also find continuation in the outdoor spaces around the house – a courtyard on the forest side and a terrace facing the sea of Skagerrak, offering a spectacular view.

The three interconnected parts of the house are adjusted to the profile of the sloping terrain, with outdoor spaces that are sheltered from the wind, while being open to the views.

"Beyond the cosiness and the strictly practical"

Cabin Nordmarka
REVER & DRAGE ARCHITECTS / 2022

Thanks to a particular foundation technique, the environmental impact of Cabin Nordmarka was reduced to steel bolts inserted into the bedrock in literally six small, drilled holes. The structure does not intervene into the terrain and can be easily removed. Rever & Drage Architects have envisioned it as a small retreat in the bolthole style. "It contains the most necessary features, but not much more. It is easy to keep clean and easy to maintain. It is light and open, but also intimate and cosy," they point out. Although the main focus has been put on the local natural environment, the architecture of the escape is itself striking. The simple pitched-roof structure is interrupted by an eye-catching corner opening, piercing the façade in a dynamic way. An ode to the view, it also gives the traditionally shaped cabin a contemporary twist.

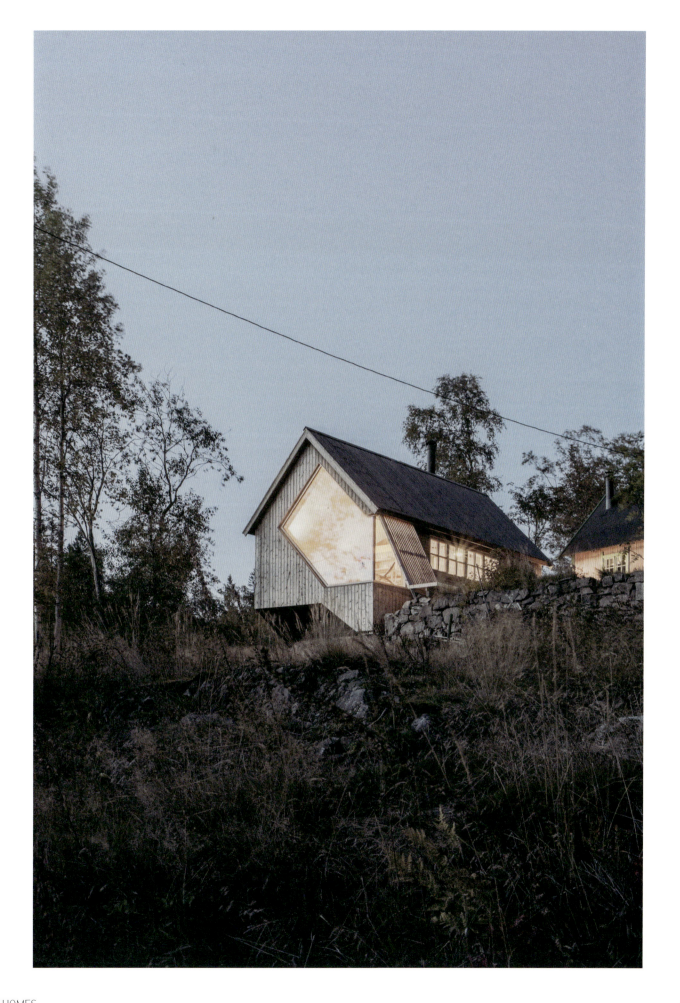

CABIN NORDMARKA

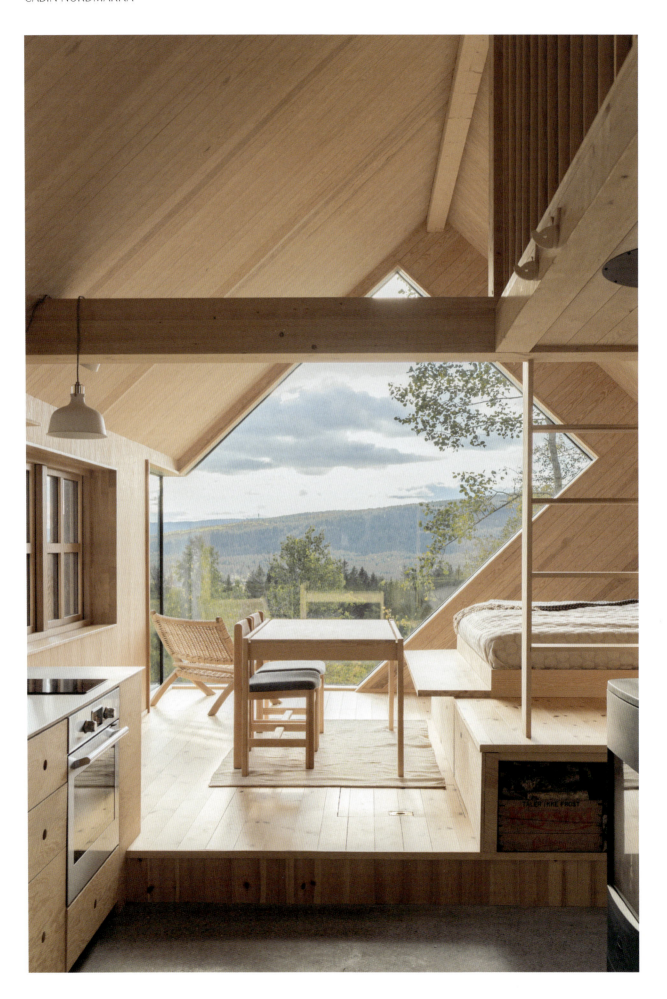

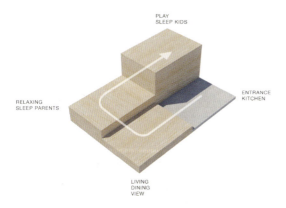

The interior is also highly affected by this grand window, as it enhances the space with a feeling of freedom and generously fills it with natural light. Designed with levels going up around the central area, quite impressively, the floor area is less than 30 square metres. Starting with the entrance and kitchen level, the living area is one step higher, while two steps further there is a relaxing space with a bed for adults, which leads up a ladder to a mezzanine space for children with both play and sleeping areas. Underneath the last part, the architects placed the bathroom as well as a storage area. Cabin Nordmarka has been erected next to a historical cabin from the 1930s and they can be used in tandem.

CABIN NORDMARKA

Nordmarka is located next to a cabin from the 1930s of similar size, which can provide additional space for living and sleeping, though it doesn't have water or electricity like the new building.

"Framing the views of an idyllic coastline"

Hytte Portør
R21 ARKITEKTER / 2021

Portør is an idyllic peninsula on the eastern coast of Norway with magnificent coves, forests and an impressive rocky shore. The scenic archipelago offers extraordinary experiences, and thus requires special consideration for any man-made structures on the coastline. The architects of R21, particularly sensitive about the context, envisioned a structure that complements the environment, striking a perfect balance with it. The house's plot has direct access to a small beach, which is an ideal bathing spot among bare rocks. Its structure, comprising two interconnected volumes, each covered with pitched roofs, sits on a concrete base fitted perfectly in between the rocks. The upper part is made of wood with a soft red hue that harmonises with the roof tiles for a monolithic effect, while contrasting with the vivid grass on the site.

HYTTE PORTØR

The spacious and bright living space is not overwhelmed with furnishings but lined entirely in warm wood, and opened up with the all-glazed façade towards the water view.

HYTTE PORTØR

> It is not only the front view that deserves attention, which is why the architects framed the scenic surroundings and created a contemplative relaxation corner with a seating area.

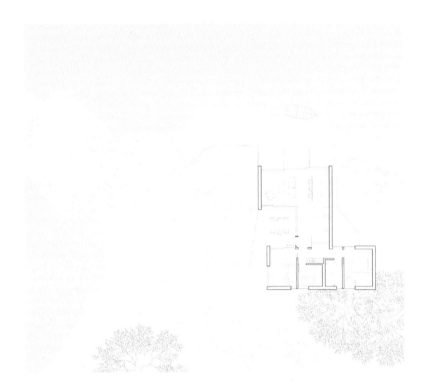

The interiors, softly enveloped with natural wood, are also filled with light, especially the main living and eating area connected to the kitchen. Here a large, glazed façade looking out onto the water is a gateway to the landscape, evoking a feeling of space and freedom. Devoid of superfluous pieces of furniture, it invites the views inside, making it part of the daily routine to feel immersed in nature. There are also more contemplative spaces throughout the house that create a special relationship with the surroundings. This is also encouraged by the outdoor areas, like an eating space sheltered from the wind. In the second volume, situated deeper into the plot, the architects planned the bedrooms and bathrooms.

"The characteristics of the site set clear premises for the project"

Villa Solveien
R21 ARKITEKTER / 2021

Villa Solveien demonstrates an inventive approach, not only to designing on a demanding plot but also to envisioning a house for a family with young children in general. Located in the Nordstrand district of Oslo, the site has a steep slope to the west with large pine trees, so it was quite a task to build a residence that would be, according to the brief, intimate and robust. "By using the site's obvious challenges as a space for opportunity, the house has gained its identity, especially through the top floor of the house," comment the architects. The access to the house leads through a bridge from the street level to the entrance hall on the top floor. From there, a spiral staircase leads downstairs to the lower levels.

VILLA SOLVEIEN

The neutral colour palette and combination of pared-down materials resulted in discreet and timeless architecture, ensuring that the landscape plays the main role and enhancing both comfort and quality of life with its minimalism.

VILLA SOLVEIEN

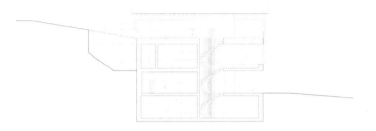

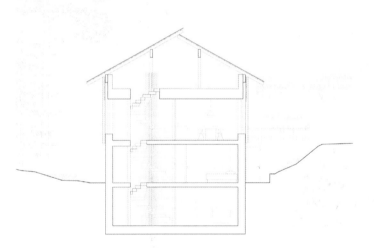

The top floor is devoted to a common social area, while the middle floor houses the main living spaces, a lounge and kitchen, and the bottom one the protectively private rooms. This division of spaces is also marked structurally – the bottom, made of solid concrete (working as an anchor in the terrain), is a protective skin for the most intimate spaces. The top floor features a lightweight wooden column structure, embracing gigantic windows and supporting the roof. This aesthetically pleasant juxtaposition of materials, timeless and elegant, has been used masterfully in this project, with intriguing results. It can be also read symbolically – the common space, engaged in a dialogue with the surroundings, is made of light and natural materials.

VILLA SOLVEIEN

Due to the topography of the terrain, the architects planned quite a unique entrance situation, where residents access the house from the street level over a bridge to a hall located just under the roof, with a spiral staircase leading down to all other spaces.

"The buildings exhibit a high degree of consistency in materials and design details"

Twin Houses
REIULF RAMSTAD ARKITEKTER / 2022

This intriguing combination of two monolithic volumes, only 20 minutes from Oslo, is a project realised by Reiulf Ramstad Arkitekter for a father and son. The idea was to create two closely located yet individual residences. The buildings' expressive look draws inspiration from local traditional boathouses. The extensively scaled windows, inserted into the façade facing the waterfront, create a stark contrast with the dark-wood structure. The volume seamlessly merges the walls, façade and roof surfaces into an elegant sculptural form. "Nestled within the picturesque rolling terrain, this project seeks to redefine coastal living by seamlessly blending with the natural surroundings and paying homage to the rich maritime history of the area," explain the architects.

TWIN HOUSES

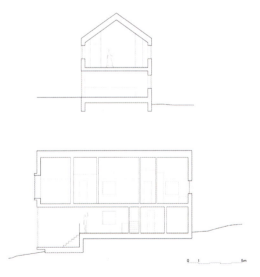

The principle in planning the floor arrangements was to maximise the utilisation of each room while also taking into consideration the plot's natural profile. The division of spaces is quite natural. An open-plan kitchen, comfortably connected with the dining area and living room, occupies the ground level, while the top floor houses private spaces. The architects used a limited set of materials, which simplified the construction process, with wood as dominant in the interiors of the house as well, only in a brighter palette of hues. The result is a spacious yet cosy interior with a good balance between the social areas, filled with light and views, and the private rooms with a more intimate atmosphere. The design was developed in 2016 and built in 2022.

TWIN HOUSES

> Despite their distinctive shape, size and colour, the Twin Houses, which flank an existing house on either side, maintain a relationship with the site – the windows on the ground level fuse the living space with the rocky terrain, while on the top floor the bedroom is visually communicated with the scenic waterfront.

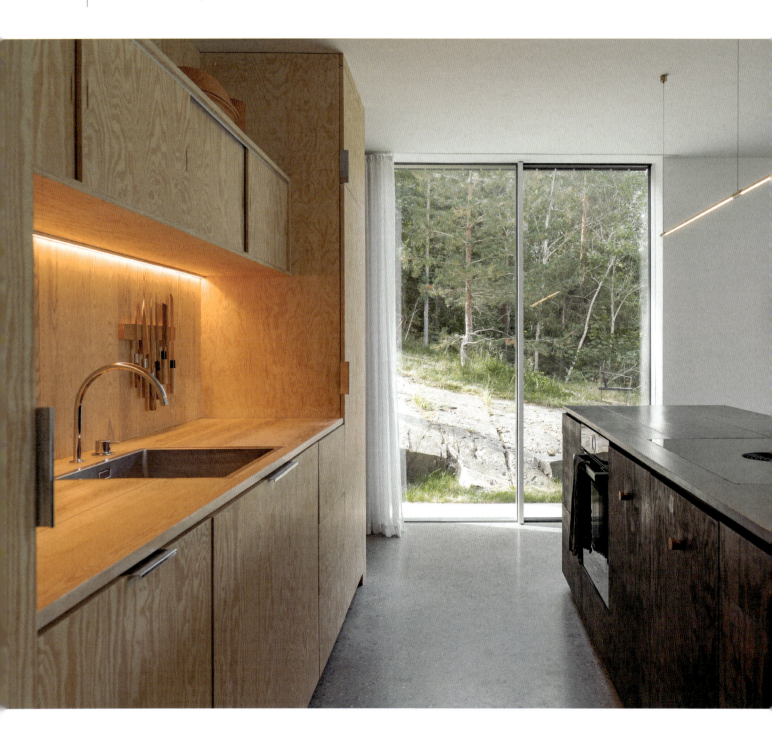

TWIN HOUSES

"The architecture is a specific response to the topography"

Woodnest
HELEN & HARD / 2020

The scenic landscape of the hillsides surrounding the Hardangerfjord is the setting for the equally unusual structures in the middle of it. Two Woodnest cabins make the childhood dream of living in a treehouse real. The structures, surrounded by trees of the surrounding forest, are located around 5 to 6 metres above the forest ground. The studio Helen & Hard envisioned micro spaces that blend perfectly into the greenery and at the same time become cosy nests for observing the surroundings. The architects' main goal was to create spaces that embody dwelling in nature. Made of a series of radial glue-laminated timber ribs, the volume is fastened to the trunk of a pine tree, which actually supports the cabin structurally.

WOODNEST

WOODNEST

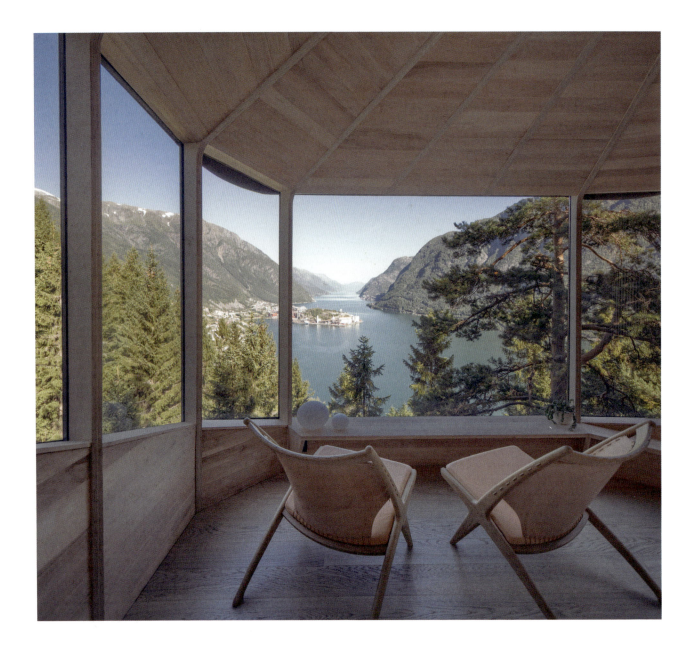

Spending a night in the Woodnest is a complex adventure including a 20-minute walk along the edge of the fjord and through the forest. The path is steep, but once visitors reach the small timber bridge leading to the door of the cabin, they quickly understand that it was worth the climb. The 15-square-metre interior has been arranged with great care for functionality, to accommodate four sleeping places, a bathroom, a kitchen area, and a living space with extraordinary views. While the interior is lined with a warm, brightly hued wood, the outer shell is covered with untreated natural timber shingles – thanks to the natural patina, these will fuse even more into the colour palette of the forest over time. The focus on timber provides not only a healthy and pleasant space for relaxation but also a unique experience for all the senses.

Like in a real nest, looking out from between the treetops, the guests can admire the breathtaking view and the way it evolves throughout the day.

NORDIC HOMES

"Beautiful deciduous forest and endless views"

Furudalen 20
KVALBEIN KORSØEN ARKITEKTUR / 2023

In the realisation of this house, the architects of the Kvalbein Korsøen Arkitektur studio looked for solutions that were far from ordinary. The Furudalen 20 house is skilfully camouflaged among the forested slopes of Nattlandsfjellet. The steepness of the hill is enhanced by the fact that the relatively large structure rests on massive pillars in the front. By anchoring the back of the volume to the rock, the architects significantly reduced the structure's impact on the natural environment. The colour of the volume matches the context through its deep green hue. Meanwhile, the shape and materials show the house's modern character, in particular, the aluminium sheets forming the outer skin – chosen for the fact that they require low maintenance – are also an original twist in harmony with the natural setting.

FURUDALEN 20

The floor-to-ceiling windows look original, both on the exteriors as well as inside the house – they create a direct relation with the context, even those located on the top floor.

The programme of the house is adjusted to the profile of the slope. The top level, connected with the top of the hill, contains the main living area with an entrance. Organised as an open space with various functions fluidly interwoven, this bright floor is enveloped by numerous large openings as well as a large terrace that all bring the extensive landscapes inside the house. The lower level, much quieter, and with fewer and smaller windows, has been dedicated to the private rooms. Both floors are communicated with a large and airy centrally located staircase. At the very bottom, under the house, a roofed area leading directly to the adjacent garden is used as a patio where the inhabitants can enjoy the outdoors even when the weather is not perfect.

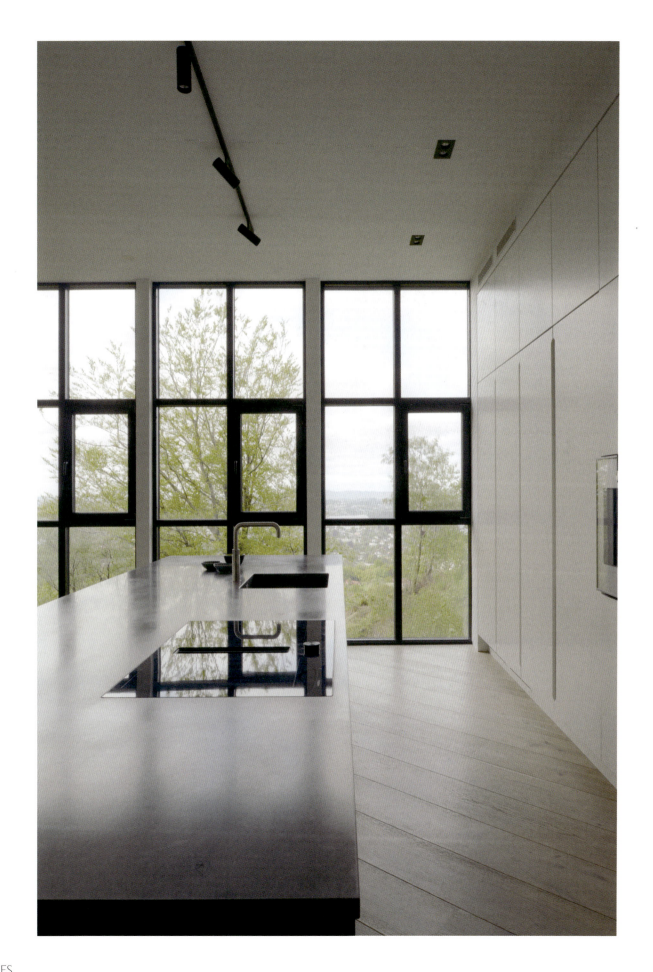

As the structure of the house is elevated, the sheltered space underneath can be used by the inhabitants as a patio with direct access to the garden.

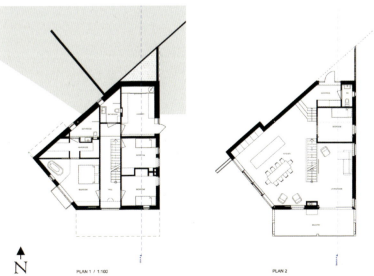

PLAN 1 / 1:100   PLAN 2

Finland

"Creating a close relationship between ecology and tectonics"

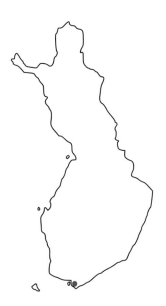

Villa Furuholmen
STRÅ ARKITEKTER + SARITA POPTANI / 2019

The main objective in this project was to create a spacious summer residence amid the unspoilt nature of an island located in the southwest archipelago of Finland without destroying its beauty. Strå Arkitekter in collaboration with Sarita Poptani created a perfect retreat that embraces the landscape. The wild vegetation, large trees and rocks have been preserved carefully. In fact, they have become the reference for the scheme of the house. "Instead of blasting the beautiful archipelago cliffs, we decided to let the typography decide the levels of the house and have it follow the terrain," they say. At the core of the concept is their decision to break up the building into several volumes, which are not posed directly on the ground but sit on stilts along a trail. They are interconnected through a series of terraces, envisioned for different uses and occasions.

VILLA FURUHOLMEN

Although the building is quite extensive, the fact that it is not very wide, nor high, visually reduces its impact on the plot, as do the simple yet dynamic shapes. This modest architectural vocabulary, together with the limited number of materials used, expresses the architects' respect for the natural surroundings. The way they draw the landscape into the interiors, which are devoid of internal corridors, also demonstrates how smooth the inside–outside relationship can be. The rooms are related to the views through significant openings, and the act of moving through the house is indeed one of experiencing the natural surroundings. This intentional lack of corridors also amplifies the space, and replacing them with outdoor spaces connects the architecture with the site even more. The interplay between the two is enhanced by the use of pine and oak in the mostly wood structure as well as surfaces with only small elements made of brick or concrete.

VILLA FURUHOLMEN

| The complex volume of the house is oriented on the plot in a way that is adjusted to the precious nature of the island – exposed cliffs and vegetation; it also makes the best of the views.

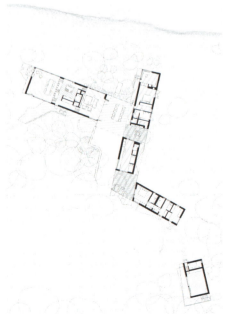

"Views of the surrounding nature are the main focus"

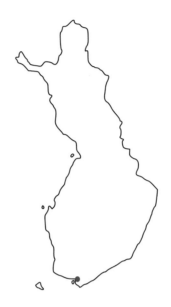

Villa Sjöviken
JENNI REUTER / 2022

"The steep site inspired me to design a building on several levels adjusted to the fragile archipelago nature," muses Jenni Reuter, the architect of this one-family home located on Kemiö island (also called Kimito island) in southern Finland. Literally immersed into the lush vegetation, the house offers inhabitants the relaxing 'forest bathing' practice as part of everyday life. The views are not limited to the wooded hill – there is also a view of the sea, which is experienced from inside the house. The building is made of wood and planned in direct relation to the topography of this unspoilt site, with even the façade cladding designed to follow the surface of the rocky foundation. It is nature that plays a major role, which the architect highlights with her restrained use of materials and colour palette.

VILLA SJÖVIKEN

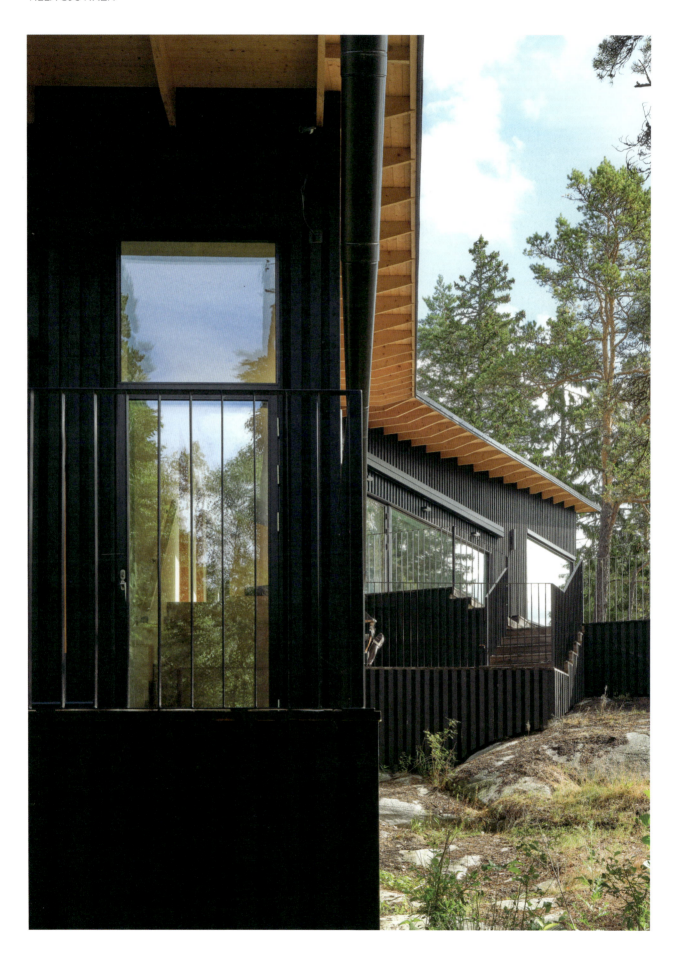

The architect planned each of three parts of the house in relation to the cliff's topography without any interventions into the land for a perfect fusion.

VILLA SJÖVIKEN

The most calming vistas of the woods and water have been framed, like this meditative corner, where the extensive opening also amplifies the interior space.

The contrast between the dark outer skin of the house and the bright interiors is striking and fulfils its role. On the one hand the presence of the volume in the context of the wooded cliff is minimised; on the other, the natural and white colours of the wood amplify the spaces inside the house. The heart of the residence is a fireplace, central to a spacious and well-lit open-plan kitchen with dining and living areas, connected to an outdoor terrace. The private rooms have been located in their own wings to clearly divide them from the social part of the house. Interestingly, all rooms are located on one floor, but due to the sloping terrain, the difference between the highest and lowest points of the structure is over 4 metres. Experiencing the interiors is thus also exploring the landscape.

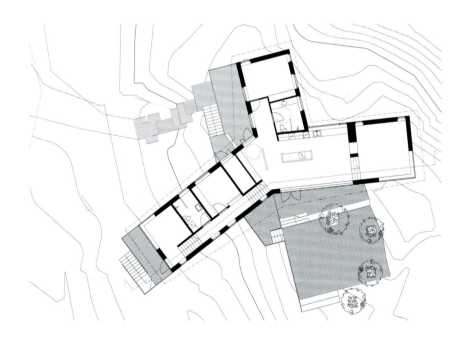

"The flattest and most scenic spot of the island"

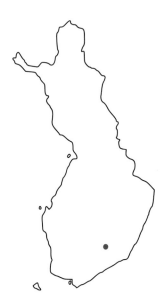

Summerhouse V
PLAYA ARCHITECTS / 2021

A small rocky island in lake Suontee in southern Finland had been a holiday spot for a family, who decided, when a small fishing cabin from the 1960s became too modest, to build a new house for the summer that would be perfectly adjusted to the island's way of life. In pursuit of the perfect plot, this one in the middle of the island was chosen for its flatness and nice views of the lake. Surrounded by old trees, the house is made entirely of wood. A non-insulated cross-laminated timber (CLT) frame was prefabricated in the shape of logs for easy transportation and assembled on site. The floor and roof have wood fibre insulation and are made of laminated veneer lumber (LVL) and glulam beams. The wood used for the building structure and interior claddings is spruce, which is intentionally untreated. Exposed to the weather, it will evolve in colour over time, coming to match the hues of the surrounding forest even more closely.

SUMMERHOUSE V

The play between open and closed in this simple yet inventive shape harmonises the volume with the site in a unique way.

SUMMERHOUSE V

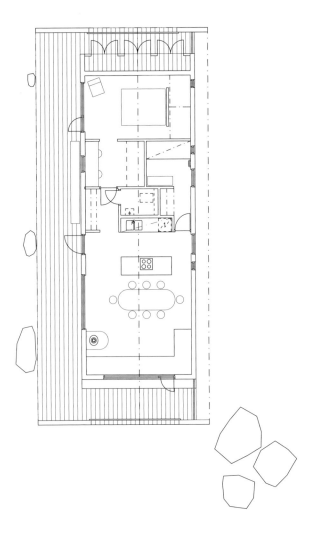

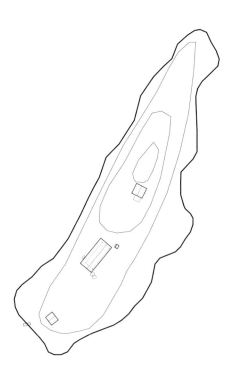

In the house's simple shape, Playa Architects demonstrate the art of building in wood, making the best of its structural and aesthetic qualities. The house's envelope is protected by a saddle roof, which is particularly visible in the main part of the interior – the kitchen connected with the living room. The interiors are completely lined in wood, which together with all the wooden furnishings creates an experience that is both tactile and nest-like. The roof's long eaves create a sheltered outdoor space around the house, which is shielded from the strong winds and makes a perfect observation point with vistas of the lake regardless of the weather.

SUMMERHOUSE V

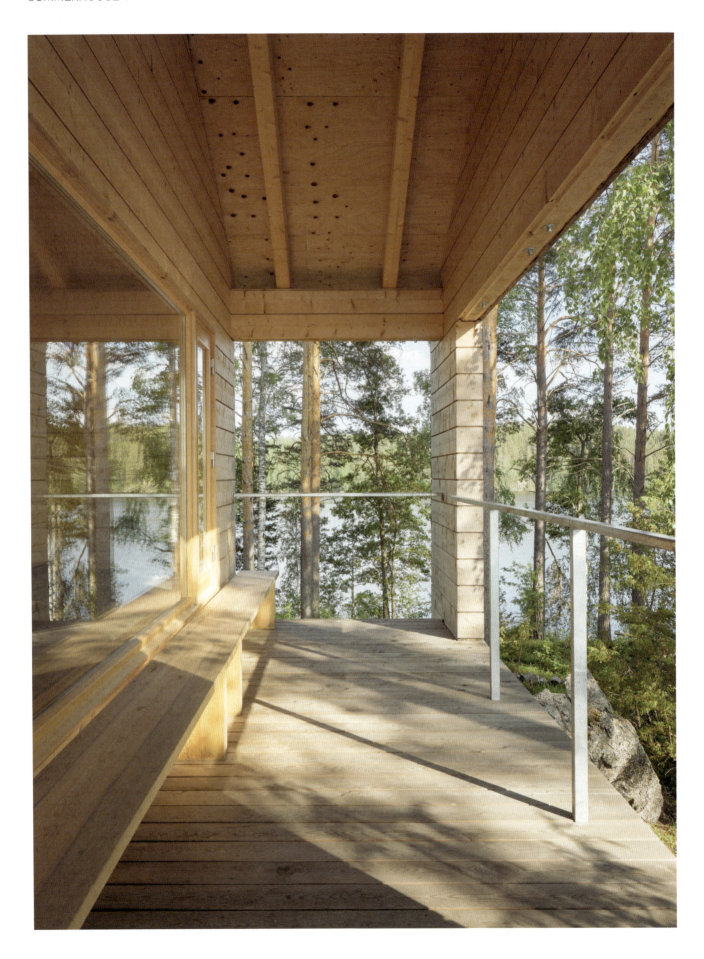

In the winter, the house owners can enjoy the landscape through large windows next to a warm chimney, and in the warmer months, from the outdoor terraces, which embrace the house and are all roofed.

"The hideaway cabin is a thought-through entity"

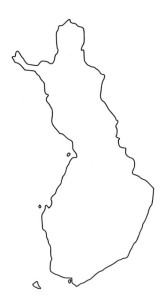

Villa K
SAUKKONEN + PARTNERS / 2020

Teemu Saukkonen, the lead designer of Saukkonen + Partners, envisioned this remotely located villa for a couple returning to Finland for occasional stays throughout the year. The unique escape retreat is adapted to all seasons, allowing the owners to admire the changing nature. All elements of this idyllic hideout have thus been planned very carefully in relation to the landscape. "The intention was to create a design that would be as maintenance-free as possible while bringing the surrounding nature into the atmosphere of the spaces," remark the architects. Paying special attention to sustainability, they made sure that all technical solutions are environmentally friendly and low in energy consumption. Durability was another aspect taken into account during the design process, while both the materials and colour palette were selected in harmony with the unspoilt nature.

VILLA K

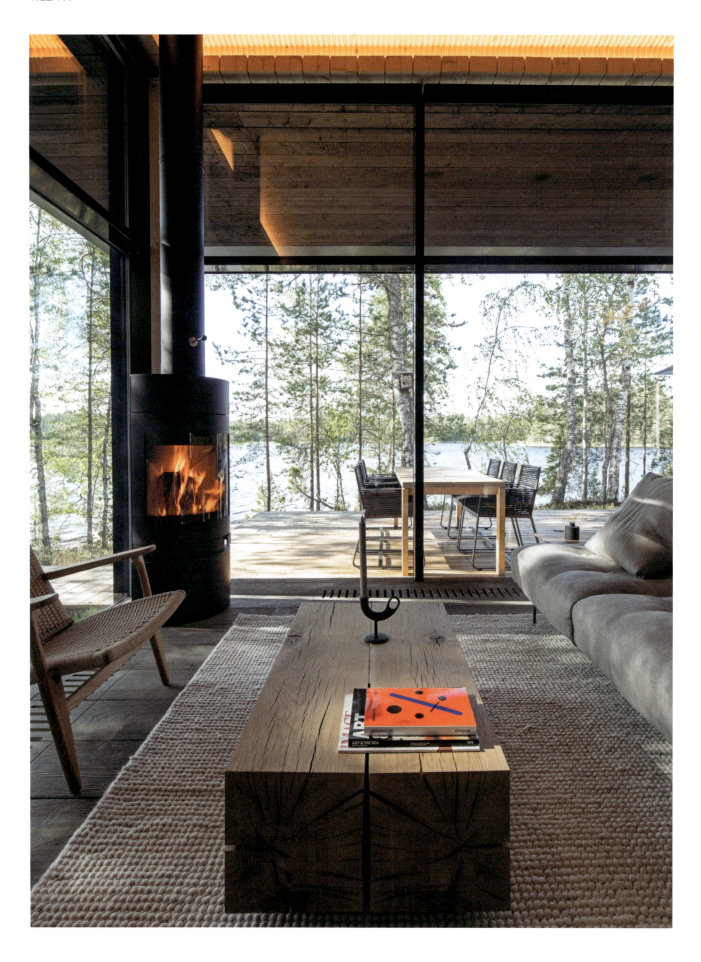

The interiors, both private and social areas, enjoy extensive views and find continuation in the outdoor spaces.

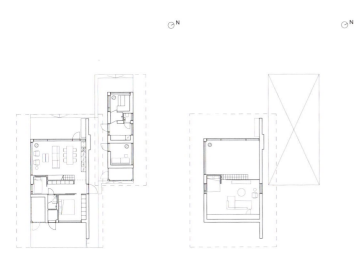

The bridge that leads from the mainland to the island is part of the design, which comprises two volumes – the main house and a separate, smaller one with a sauna. The two are linked by their overlapping roof structures. The bird's-eye view, in particular, shows that this structure is positioned in a harmonious way within the vegetation on site, which was the architects' main ambition. They wished to avoid overpowering the landscape, and achieved this with a nicely scaled wooden structure, adjusted to the island's topography. The interiors are defined by extensive openings – the programme of the house was planned around the views of the lake to the west, and from the main living area the inhabitants can enjoy the sunset in the evenings.

VILLA K

The way Villa K is positioned in the landscape of the remote island, on a lake in Finland, makes the best of its direct proximity to water.

"A collective holiday home intricately tailored to the site"

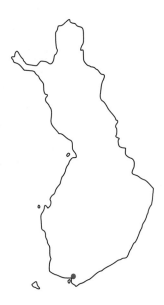

Two Sisters Holiday Home
MNY ARKITEKTER / 2023

Two Sisters Holiday Home was designed by MNY Arkitekter studio for two siblings and their families, with the main principle of 'together separately' in mind. The context of the rocky site and pine forest as well as the nearby sea makes a scenic background for this quintessential summer residence, which imposed another goal – constructing a villa that would preserve the beautiful pine trees on the site. The architects used massive wood for this complex structure, which not only harmonises the house with the surroundings but also creates the immersive atmosphere of a holiday cabin. Incorporating the buildings that were pre-existing on the site, a sauna and a shelter, made the layout of the retreat even more original. As a result, it is divided into four smaller volumes of different heights, which enhances the effect of blending them into the landscape.

TWO SISTERS HOLIDAY HOME

The hideout has two separate units with a narrow entrance in between them and extensive shared terraces. "The fan-shaped form and functional duality of the building create captivating views and spaces throughout," remark the architects. Interestingly, inside each of the volumes, the other unit is barely visible except from one window seat, yet all interiors have stunning views of the surrounding environment. In the bright interiors, only dark fixed furniture, mainly in the kitchen, and a black fireplace create visual accents. The wooden structural frame of the house was prefabricated and covered with spruce cladding, while the floor and roof are made of glulam beams with recycled wood fibre insulation. Structural elements are beautifully exposed to highlight the woodwork – the roof beams and the meticulous wood cladding in the rooms add to the summery spirit.

TWO SISTERS HOLIDAY HOME

The box-like interiors are lined with wood on all surfaces, which creates a tactile experience but also visually merges the rooms with the pine forest beyond the windows.

Index

INDEX

NAME: SKAGEN KLITGÅRD
LOCATION: SKAGEN, DENMARK
COMPLETION YEAR: 2021
ARCHITECTS: PAX ARCHITECTS
PHOTOGRAPHER: RASMUS HJORTSHØJ
PAGES: 10-17

NAME: KILDESKOVSVEJ
LOCATION: KILDESKOVSVEJ, GENTOFTE, DENMARK
COMPLETION YEAR: 2023
ARCHITECTS: VALBÆK BRØRUP ARCHITECTS
PHOTOGRAPHER: PETER KRAGBALLE
PAGES: 18-25

NAME: HEATHERHILL BEACH HOUSE
LOCATION: VEJBY, DENMARK
COMPLETION YEAR: 2024
ARCHITECTS: NORM ARCHITECTS
PHOTOGRAPHER: JONAS BJERRE-POULSEN
PAGES: 26-33

NAME: VIPP COLD HAWAII GUESTHOUSE
LOCATION: THY, DENMARK
COMPLETION YEAR: 2024
ARCHITECTS: HAHN LAVSEN
PHOTOGRAPHER: PIA WINTHER (PP. 35-39),
MARTIN HOFFMANN LARSEN (PP. 40-41)
PAGES: 34-41

NAME: LYSAL PAVILION
LOCATION: LUNDBY KRAT, DENMARK
COMPLETION YEAR: 2023
ARCHITECTS: N+P ARKITEKTUR
PHOTOGRAPHER: JESPER KORF
PAGES: 42-47

NAME: VILLA STRÖMMA
LOCATION: STOCKHOLM, STRÖMMA, SWEDEN
COMPLETION YEAR: 2022
ARCHITECTS: ANDRÉNFOGELSTRÖM
PHOTOGRAPHER: NADJA ENDLER
PAGES: 50-55

NAME: VILLA TIMMERMAN
LOCATION: GOTHENBURG, SWEDEN
COMPLETION YEAR: 2020
ARCHITECTS: ANDREAS LYCKEFORS + JOSEFINE WIKHOLM
PHOTOGRAPHER: KALLE SANNER
PAGES: 56-63

NAME: HOLIDAY HOME
LOCATION: THE ARCHIPELAGO OF STOCKHOLM, SWEDEN
COMPLETION YEAR: 2019
ARCHITECTS: MARGEN WIGOW ARKITEKTKONTOR
PHOTOGRAPHER: ÅKE E:SON LINDMAN
PAGES: 64-71

NAME: SUMMERHOUSE SOLVIKEN
LOCATION: MÖLLE, SWEDEN
COMPLETION YEAR: 2018
ARCHITECTS: JOHAN SUNDBERG ARKITEKTUR
PHOTOGRAPHER: PEO OLSSON
PAGES: 72-79

NAME: YNGSJÖ
LOCATION: YNGSJÖ, SWEDEN
COMPLETION YEAR: 2023
ARCHITECTS: JOHAN SUNDBERG ARKITEKTUR
PHOTOGRAPHER: MARKUS LINDEROTH
PAGES: 80-85

NAME: FIELD HOUSE
LOCATION: FÅRÖ ISLAND, SWEDEN
COMPLETION YEAR: 2020
ARCHITECTS: LOOKOFSKY ARCHITECTURE
PHOTOGRAPHER: MATTIAS HAMRÉN
PAGES: 86-93

NAME: DALARÖ HOUSE
LOCATION: THE STOCKHOLM ARCHIPELAGO, SWEDEN
COMPLETION YEAR: 2019
ARCHITECTS: OLSON KUNDIG
PHOTOGRAPHER: MAGNUS MÅRDING
PAGES: 94-99

NAME: SJÖPARKEN
LOCATION: HALLAND, SWEDEN
COMPLETION YEAR: 2024
ARCHITECTS: NORM ARCHITECTS
PHOTOGRAPHER: JONAS BJERRE-POULSEN
PAGES: 100 -107

NAME: HOUSE ON A HILL
LOCATION: OUTSKIRTS OF STOCKHOLM, SWEDEN
COMPLETION YEAR: 2022
ARCHITECTS: THAM & VIDEGÅRD ARKITEKTER
PHOTOGRAPHER: ÅKE E:SON LINDMAN
PAGES: 108-115

NAME: LIBRARY HOUSE
LOCATION: STOCKHOLM, SWEDEN
COMPLETION YEAR: 2022
ARCHITECTS: FRIA FOLKET, HANNA MICHELSON
PHOTOGRAPHER: HANNA MICHELSON
PAGES: 116-123

NAME: SIMONSSON HOUSE
LOCATION: BODEN, SWEDEN
COMPLETION YEAR: 2021
ARCHITECTS: CLAESSON KOIVISTO RUNE ARCHITECTS
PHOTOGRAPHER: ÅKE E:SON LINDMAN
PAGES: 124-131

NAME: JOHÄLL GETAWAY HOUSE
LOCATION: BORÅS, SWEDEN
COMPLETION YEAR: 2024
ARCHITECTS: CLAESSON KOIVISTO RUNE ARCHITECTS
PHOTOGRAPHER: ÅKE E:SON LINDMAN
PAGES: 132-139

NAME: SOUTH LOFT
LOCATION: VALLSTA, SWEDEN
COMPLETION YEAR: 2021
ARCHITECTS: FRIA FOLKET, HANNA MICHELSON
PHOTOGRAPHER: HANNA MICHELSON
PAGES: 140-147

NAME: SALTVIGA HOUSE
LOCATION: GRIMSTAD, NORWAY
COMPLETION YEAR: 2022
ARCHITECTS: KOLMAN BOYE ARCHITECTS
PHOTOGRAPHER: JOHAN DEHLIN
PAGES: 150-155

NAME: CABIN NORDMARKA
LOCATION: NORDMARKA - OSLO, NORWAY
COMPLETION YEAR: 2022
ARCHITECTS: REVER & DRAGE ARCHITECTS
PHOTOGRAPHER: TOM AUGER
PAGES: 156-163

NAME: HYTTE PORTØR
LOCATION: KRAGERØ, NORWAY
COMPLETION YEAR: 2021
ARCHITECTS: R21 ARKITEKTER
PHOTOGRAPHER: RUBEN RATKUSIC
PAGES: 164-171

NAME: VILLA SOLVEIEN
LOCATION: NORDSTRAND, OSLO, NORWAY
COMPLETION YEAR: 2021
ARCHITECTS: R21 ARKITEKTER
PHOTOGRAPHER: MARIELA APOLLONIO
PAGES: 172-179

NAME: TWIN HOUSES
LOCATION: NÆRSNES, NORWAY
COMPLETION YEAR: 2022
ARCHITECTS: REIULF RAMSTAD ARKITEKTER
PHOTOGRAPHER: KRISTIAN AALERUD
PAGES: 180-187

NAME: WOODNEST
LOCATION: ODDA, NORWAY
COMPLETION YEAR: 2020
ARCHITECTS: HELEN & HARD
PHOTOGRAPHER: SINDRE ELLINGSEN
PAGES: 188-195

NAME: FURUDALEN 20
LOCATION: BERGEN, NORWAY
COMPLETION YEAR: 2023
ARCHITECTS: KVALBEIN KORSØEN ARKITEKTUR
PHOTOGRAPHER: KVALBEIN KORSØEN ARKITEKTUR
PAGES: 196-201

NAME: VILLA FURUHOLMEN
LOCATION: KIMITO, FINLAND
COMPLETION YEAR: 2019
ARCHITECTS: STRÅ ARKITEKTER + SARITA POPTANI
PHOTOGRAPHER: THURSTON EMPSON
PAGES: 204-209

NAME: VILLA SJÖVIKEN
LOCATION: KEMIÖ ISLAND, FINLAND
COMPLETION YEAR: 2022
ARCHITECTS: JENNI REUTER
PHOTOGRAPHER: MARC GOODWIN
PAGES: 210-217

NAME: SUMMERHOUSE V
LOCATION: HIRVENSALMI, FINLAND
COMPLETION YEAR: 2021
ARCHITECTS: PLAYA ARCHITECTS
PHOTOGRAPHER: TUOMAS UUSHEIMO
PAGES: 218-227

NAME: VILLA K
LOCATION: FINLAND
COMPLETION YEAR: 2020
ARCHITECTS: SAUKKONEN + PARTNERS
PHOTOGRAPHER: TIMO PYYKÖNEN
PAGES: 228-235

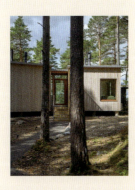

NAME: TWO SISTERS HOLIDAY HOME
LOCATION: SALO, FINLAND
COMPLETION YEAR: 2023
ARCHITECTS: MNY ARKITEKTER
PHOTOGRAPHER: MULTIFOTO AB
PAGES: 236-243

WEBSITES

ANDREAS LYCKEFORS + JOSEFINE WIKHOLM   olssonlyckefors.se
ANDRÉNFOGELSTRÖM   andrenfogelstrom.se
CLAESSON KOIVISTO RUNE ARCHITECTS   claessonkoivistorune.se
FRIA FOLKET + HANNA MICHELSON   friafolket.se
HAHN LAVSEN   hahnlavsen.dk
HELEN & HARD   helenhard.no
JENNI REUTER   jennireuter.fi
JOHAN SUNDBERG ARKITEKTUR   johansundberg.com
KOLMAN BOYE ARCHITECTS   kolmanboye.se
KVALBEIN KOROEN ARKITEKTUR   kvalbeinarkitektur.no
LOOKOFSKY ARCHITECTURE   lookofskyarch.com
MARGEN WIGOW ARKITEKTKONTOR   margenwigow.se
METTE LANGE ARCHITECTS   mettelange.com
MNY ARKITEKTER   mnyark.fi
N+P ARKITEKTUR   nplusp.dk
NORM ARCHITECTS   normcph.com
OLSON KUNDIG   olsonkundig.com
PAX ARCHITECTS   pax.dk
PLAYA ARCHITECTS   playa.fi
R21 ARKITEKTER   r21.no
REIULF RAMSTAD ARKITEKTER   reiulframstadarkitekter.com
REVER & DRAGE ARCHITECTS   reverdrage.no
SAUKKONEN + PARTNERS   saukkonenpartners.fi
STRÅ ARKITEKTER + SARITA POPTANI   straaa.com   saritapoptani.com
THAM & VIDEGÅRD   thamvidegard.se
VALBÆK BRØRUP ARCHITECTS   vba.dk

PHOTO CREDITS

Front cover:
© Kolman Boye Architects, photography © Johan Dehlin
Back cover:
© THAM & VIDEGÅRD ARKITEKTER, photography © Åke E:son Lindman
Front endpapers:
© VIPP A/S, photography © Pia Winther
Back endpapers:
© NORM ARCHITECTS, photography © Jonas Bjerre-Poulsen

Pp.:
11-17 © PAX ARCHITECTS, photography © Rasmus Hjortshøj; Drawing p. 17 © PAX ARCHITECTS

19-25 © VALBÆK BRØRUP ARCHITECTS, photography © Peter Kragballe; Plan p. 23 © Valbæk Brørup Architects

7, 27-33, 101-107 © NORM ARCHITECTS, photography © Jonas Bjerre-Poulsen

35-39 © VIPP A/S, HANH LAVSEN, photography © Pia Winther
2, 40-41 © VIPP A/S, HANH LAVSEN, photography © Martin Hoffmann Larsen

43-46 © N+P ARKITEKTUR, photography © Jesper Korf; Plan p. 47 © N+P ARKITEKTUR

51-53, 55 © AndrénFogelström, photography © Nadja Endler; Plan and drawings p. 54 © AndrénFogelström

4, 57-62 © Andreas Lyckefors + Josefine Wikholm, photography © Kalle Sanner; Plans p. 63 © Andreas Lyckefors + Josefine Wikholm

65-71 © MARGEN WIGOW ARKITEKTKONTOR, photography © Åke E:son Lindman; Drawing p. 67 and plan p. 69 © MARGEN WIGOW ARKITEKTKONTOR

73-79 © Johan Sundberg ARKITEKTUR, photography © Peo Olsson
81-85 © Johan Sundberg ARKITEKTUR, photography © Markus Linderoth

87-93 © David Lookofsky / Lookofsky Architecture, photography © Mattias Hamrén; Plan p. 91 © David Lookofsky / Lookofsky Architecture

95-99 © Olson Kundig, photography © Magnus Mårding

109-115 © THAM & VIDEGÅRD ARKITEKTER, photography © Åke E:son Lindman; Plans p. 110 and drawings p. 113 © THAM & VIDEGÅRD ARKITEKTER

117-123, 141-147 © Fria Folket, Hanna Michelson, photography © Hanna Michelson; Plans pp. 123, 145 and drawings p. 147 © Fria Folket, Hanna Michelson

125-139 © CLAESSON KOIVISTO RUNE ARCHITECTS, photography © Åke E:son Lindman; Plans pp. 127, 137 and drawings pp. 128, 134 © CLAESSON KOIVISTO RUNE ARCHITECTS

151-155 © Kolman Boye Architects, photography © Johan Dehlin; Drawing p. 155 © Kolman Boye Architects

157-163 © Rever & Drage Architects, photography © Tom Auger; Drawing p. 159 © Rever & Drage Architects

165-171 © R21 Arkitekter, photography © Ruben Ratkusic;
173-179 © R21 Arkitekter, photography © Mariela Apollonio; Plan p. 168 and drawings p. 177 © R21 Arkitekter

181-187 © REIULF RAMSTAD ARKITEKTER, photography © Kristian Aalerud; Drawings p. 183 REIULF RAMSTAD ARKITEKTER

189-195 © Helen & Hard, photography © Sindre Ellingsen

197-201 © KVALBEIN KORSØEN ARKITEKTUR; Plans p. 201 © KVALBEIN KORSØEN ARKITEKTUR

205-209 © STRÅ Arkitekter, photography © Thurston Empson; Drawing p. 207 and plan p. 208 © STRÅ Arkitekter

211-217 © Jenni Reuter Architects, photography © Marc Goodwin; Plan p. 215 © Jenni Reuter Architects

219-227 © Playa Architects, photography © TUOMAS UUSHEIMO; Plan and drawing p. 222 © Playa Architects

229-235 © Teemu Saukkonen / SAUKKONEN + PARTNERS, photography © Timo Pyykönen; Plans p. 231 © Teemu Saukkonen / SAUKKONEN + PARTNERS

237-243 © MNY ARKITEKTER, photography Multifoto AB

Index pp. 246-253 All copyrights as mentioned above.

Chapter openers, pp.:
8-9 photography © Esther Höfling / Pexels; 48-49 photography © Efrem Efre / Pexels; 148-149 photography © stein egil liland / Pexels; 202-203 photography © Olivier Darny / Pexels; 244-245 photography © Nico Becker / Pexels

Text and Graphic Design: Agata Toromanoff, Fancy Books Packaging
Copy-editing: Allison Adelman

© Lannoo Publishers, Belgium, 2024
D/2024/45/186 - NUR 640/648
ISBN: 978 94 014 1763 1

www.lannoo.com

If you have any questions or comments about the material in this book, please do not hesitate to contact our editorial team: art@lannoo.com

All rights reserved. No part of this publication may be reproduced or transmitted in any form or by any means, electronic or mechanical, including photography, recording or any other information storage and retrieval system, without prior permission in writing from the publisher.